RAISING
CHASTE
CATHOLIC MEN

Practical Advice, Mom to Mom

Leila Miller

HOLY HEROES BOOKS · CRAMERTON, NORTH CAROLINA

Catechism quotations are taken from the *Catechism of the Catholic Church* (2nd Edition). Washington, DC: Libreria Editrice Vaticana—United States Conference of Catholic Bishops, ©2000.

Scripture quotations are taken from the New Revised Standard Version, Catholic Edition, ©1989, 1993, Division of Christian Education of the National Council of Churches of Christ in the United States of America. Used by permission. All rights reserved.

Anthony Esolen's essay, "Talk to your father" originally appeared in *Crisis Magazine* online, October 25, 2017 (crisismagazine.com/2017/tak-to-your-father). Used with permission.

Cover and book design by Chris Pelicano.
Cover photo, "Stopping to visit Jesus," ©2016 Beth Pack.

Published in the United States by
Holy Heroes, LLC
P.O. Box 12
Cramerton, NC 28032
1-855-Try-2B-Holy (855-879-2246)
HolyHeroes.com

Raising Chaste Catholic Men / Leila Miller —2nd Edition.
ISBN 978-1-936330-78-2

Dedication

To my parents, Dr. Farouk and Mary Habra,
who chose life for me twice, in birth and in baptism.
I cannot thank them enough for all they have done for me.

To my beloved cousin and friend, Michelle Jean Habra,
who left us for her true Home on April 13, 2015.
Her passion for the moral formation of her children
rivaled my own.

And to the Blessed Mother,
who took me under her mantle when I was little,
waited patiently for me when I strayed,
and has never let go of my hand
since I returned to the Church.
She teaches us all how to conform our lives
to her Divine Son:
"Do whatever He tells you."

Contents

Foreword
Jason Evert

I magine doing all you could to raise your son in the Catholic Faith, only to have him abandon the Church, father a child out of wedlock, and become involved in astrology. To make matters worse, imagine learning that he was preparing to sail overseas to pursue his career, despite your pleas for him to stay. When the time came for his departure, he assured you that he had no such plans to leave, and invited you to spend the night in a nearby chapel. By the time you awoke, he was gone.

Sounds like quite a brat.

Well, today we know this young man as Saint Augustine, whose conversion was largely due to the tireless intercession of his mother, Saint Monica. In his words, "I surrendered myself entirely to lust." However, his mother "wept to [God] for me more bitterly than mothers weep for the bodily deaths of their children." In the midst of her agony, a holy bishop assured her that "as sure as you live, it is impossible that the son of these tears should perish." Despite the seventeen years he spent resisting grace, her prayers proved to be more stubborn than his vices.

Although the drama of his conversion unfolded 1600 years ago, mothers down through the centuries have always related to Monica's trials. However, something today is different. Raising a family in the year 400 probably wasn't much different from raising a family in the year 1400, but raising a child today looks nothing like it did even twenty-five years ago. In many ways, parents today are pioneers, traversing an uncharted frontier of parenthood. From the challenges of sexting and internet porn to the relentless attacks on marriage and the meaning of "gender," parents face an endless array of forces that oppose the values they hope to instill in their children. But as difficult and frustrating as our modern situation may be, God promises that where sin abounds, grace abounds all the more (Rom. 5:20)!

Though we may be tempted to remove our families from the world and move to a desert island or an isolated rural compound, this isn't the solution. Instead of being afraid of what the world could do to our children, we ought to have bold confidence in what our children are going to do for the world. They need to see this hope in our eyes. As St. Paul exhorted Timothy, "God did not give us a spirit of timidity but a spirit of power and love and self-control" (2 Tim 1:7).

In this book, you will find practical strategies for empowering the boys in your family to become the men that God has created them to be. Having raised several sons, Leila Miller speaks from experience and with great compassion. She knows the challenges every mother faces, and offers a clear path for leading sons to become the leaders that God has created them to be. My prayer is that this book will be a blessing for you and your children, so that they (and you) can become the saints that families, centuries from now, will look to for inspiration.

Jason Evert
chastityproject.com
Author of *Raising Pure Teens*
May 1, 2018

Foreword
Father Dwight Longenecker

The question I ask many young men in their twenties is, "What are you going to do with the precious life God has given you?"

They are good, faithful Catholics, but many of them have lost the sense of vocation, and I explain to them that men need a vocation. We need something to live for and something to die for. That "something" is our Catholic faith, but in our modern, confused, materialistic society, many young men don't know how to find a true vocation.

Society tells them they must simply make as much money as possible, have as much fun as possible, and spin out their boyhood as long as possible.

In the meantime, God is calling them to grow up into the full manhood of Jesus Christ.

In times gone the way to do this was obvious: you were either a priest or brother or you were a husband and father. Life was hard and truth was sharp. By the time you were in your twenties, you had to make up your mind and go for it. Now, for many young men, it is possible to postpone adulthood for another five years. A recent study suggested that adolescence for most American men lasts until they are twenty-five.

If a man in his mid-twenties is to make a strong decision to either be a priest or be a husband and father, he needs a firm foundation on which to make that decision. The firm foundation is not only one of clear catechesis and sound establishment in the faith—it also needs to be a firm foundation in self-discipline and chastity. This firm foundation helps to keep the right priorities before a young man—so that he sees clearly and can stay on the right track—and if he stumbles and falls, he realizes that he must get up, dust himself off, and keep going.

Leila Miller's book provides practical advice in laying that foundation, helping young men navigate the perils of popular culture, pornography, gender confusion, and the complicated adventure of becoming strong, vital, and dynamic men.

Our Western society is wallowing in decadence, selfishness, violence, and perversion. Those who are locked into these lifestyles are desperately lost, often in a downward spiral of hopelessness, cynicism, atheism, and despair. Families are broken, hearts are broken, marriages are broken, and communities are broken.

In our increasingly mobile, fractured, and disjointed world, the need for strong men and women to establish truly Christian marriages and families is greater than ever before. It is only through a firm commitment to true chastity and faithful marriage or celibacy that the human person can truly flourish and establish such families and Christian communities.

As an increasing number of young men and women choose to do so, they will be the seedlings of a new Christian civilization that is founded on true love, true faith, true abundance, and true human integrity.

Father Dwight Longenecker
Catholic Priest, Author, Speaker
May 1, 2018

Acknowledgments

The Good Lord knows I couldn't do any writing, much less write an entire book, without lots of help and encouragement!

First, I pour out my undying love and gratitude to my husband Dean, who does more in one day that I do in a week, and who always picks up the slack when I let things drop. I specifically want to thank him for not getting mad when I typed and typed on a glowing computer into the wee hours of the morning and in the same room where he was trying to sleep (usually with a blindfold and occasionally with earplugs).

A shout out to my wonderful children, who have humored me... er, cheered me on through my blogging adventures and then into the wild world of writing books. Thank you for loving and embracing the precious gift of your Catholic faith.

I am grateful to the incredible ladies who helped me with this second edition: Megan Stout, Elizabeth Boyko, and Beth Pack (the photographer whose adorable son graces the book's cover). And although he's certainly no lady, Ken Davison of Holy Heroes gets a huge thank you, too, as he saw the book's worth and approached me about publishing this expanded and improved volume. I am truly humbled.

To everyone who has befriended me, followed my work, and encouraged me over the years, I thank you for all the support, friendship, and kindness you've shown me. You all are the best, and you continue to motivate and inspire me. I especially appreciate all of your prayers.

Finally, I'd like to express my deepest gratitude to my own beloved shepherd, Bishop Thomas J. Olmsted of Phoenix, for taking the crisis of manhood seriously by writing *Into the Breach: An Apostolic Exhortation to Catholic Men* that inspired much of this book.

Leila Miller
May 1, 2018

Introduction

On the Feast of the Archangels, September 29, 2015, Phoenix Bishop Thomas J. Olmsted promulgated *Into the Breach: An Apostolic Exhortation to Catholic Men.*[1] As the mother of many sons, one particular line jumped out at me and grabbed me by the lapels:

> Imagine standing before the throne of God on judgment day, where the great saints of ages past, who themselves dealt with preeminent sins in their own day, will say to each other, "We dealt with the trouble of lust in our day, but those 21st century men! These happy few battled the beast up close!"

The sexual sins are the sins of our day. There is no denying it, and there is no denying that our men and boys struggle mightily to remain chaste and retain their purity in a world designed to incite lust and drag them down to the dark pit of hell.

Dramatic? Nope. It's just reality. Sin is real, hell is real, and the temptation surrounding our sons is real. Far from suggesting that we become apathetic or despairing, I am incredibly hopeful and confident that our boys can avoid the sins of unchastity and thrive as healthy, unaddicted, free men of God, ready to lead their families as devout and honorable husbands and fathers one day or to lead the faithful as holy priests. This is no pipe dream, as I see it happening all around me.

Over the years, several Catholic mothers have come to me asking for help. Specifically, they wanted me to write something on raising up "good Catholic men" or "real Catholic men" in this corrosive culture. In early 2016, I received two message requests in two days from two amazing Catholic women whom I greatly admire (ahem, Amy and Katie), and it suddenly hit me that it was time to start writing. The response to the first, self-published edition that came out later that year has been so positive that here we find ourselves with a second edition.

The level of worry out there is high, and if you are reading this, you are probably at least a little bit concerned yourself. My friend Beth Pack (who shot the cover photo for this book, with her son as the model) told me, "This is the thing I am most worried about with my kids. Porn and sexual sins destroy lives."

Catholic mothers feel inadequate, helpless, and even hopeless about the onslaught that their boys will face as they leave the safety of their homes and face the outside world.

By the grace of God alone, I have been spared that particular worry. When my husband, Dean, and I were hit with the truth and beauty of human sexuality and conformed our lives to it (six years and three children into our marriage), my confidence soared. This makes sense! This is clear! This works! This is truth!

Perhaps my confidence was naïve, but so far it has been justified: Our oldest three boys (and two daughters) have grown through and past adolescence, and all have keep the Faith. The signs are the same for the three boys just behind them.

This is *not* a pat on my own back. It's a humble and joyful acknowledgment that God is sovereign and His design for us is perfect. He is bigger than this culture, and we need to have faith, hope, and trust that His promises are real and transformative. Divine grace is not fairy dust or some imaginary, nebulous, "feel good" construct. Grace is real, and it is powerful. It is the very life of God dwelling within us, and when we have the gift of that grace, we can act with heroic virtue—an ultimately attractive thing for boys and men, whose desire for heroism is hardwired into them by their Creator.

I want you to hear in this book that I am no different from you, and your boys are no different from mine. You *can* do this. Do not fear, and do not be anxious! If you live in accordance with Catholic teaching and fully assent to the sexual moral law, it is possible to form your sons to be chaste and free, not slaves to sin. Remember that God has adequately equipped you to be an effective and fruitful parent. He has given you all the tools you need, and, with His grace, you can help your boys to be who He created them to be.

This book will be a practical guide for what that journey might entail and how to prepare your sons to "battle the beast up close."

Onward! . . .

Chapter One

What This Book Is *Not*

Okay my friends, before we dive in, I want to tell you what this book is *not*.

This is not a general Catholic parenting book. Others have done that and done it well.

This is not a book about teaching manners, or social graces, or any of life's niceties (of which I am very much in favor, by the way).

This is not a book about how to raise Catholic gentleman per se, although I have said more times than I can count, "I will raise Catholic gentlemen if it kills me!" But while not about raising gentlemen generally, this or any book promoting male chastity will touch upon it, because chastity and gentlemanliness coincide.

This is not a book on the basics of Catholic teaching. Although this is a Catholic book, both the discussion and advice herein *presuppose* that you are already a practicing, faithful Catholic and that your children are being raised in the Catholic faith. It *presupposes* that you are teaching your children about God the Father, Son, and Holy Spirit, about the Incarnation of Jesus Christ, His teachings, His miracles, His Mother Mary, His Church and the sacraments He established, His Passion, atoning death on the Cross, and bodily Resurrection, the Communion of Saints, the absolute necessity of Scripture and prayer, etc.

You should be reading "Jesus, prayer, sacraments" between every line. If you aren't doing that part, the advice here will not be effective. I also pray that you have at least an elemental understanding of the truth and meaning of human sexuality and Theology of the Body, but if not, check the Appendix for resources.

This is not a book about raising daughters in a pornified culture, although my husband and I have raised two chaste daughters, both grown and married now, and there are many points from this book that can apply to girls as well. However, considering the current crisis of manhood and the number of Catholic moms who have asked me specifically about raising good Catholic men, I am making boys the focus of this volume.

This is not a book that represents, denies, or usurps the father's role in the life of a boy/teen/young man. The importance of a father in a young man's life cannot be overstated. Fathers and other male role models are *crucial* for forming boys into good men. However, the only people who have asked me to write on this subject are women, and it's something I can approach only from a woman's perspective (for obvious biological reasons). My husband is not a writer, so his book on this subject will never materialize, but he's fully on board with all that I am writing here (thank you, Honey!).

This is not an exhaustive treatment of the subject matter, not by a long shot. So very much more can and should be said, and yet I know that my readers are busy moms with very little time to spend on a book. I wanted to make this as short and sweet (and practical) as possible.

This is not a book of new revelation or ideas. You may find yourself nodding your head as you read along. You likely could have written this book yourself, because what is contained herein is pretty much common sense. It's important to have reinforcement and encouragement, though, from other moms who understand. These words will not blow you away as if you are learning something brand new, but they will confirm you in what you are already doing or want to be doing. They will remind you that you don't have to be reactionary or have freak-outs simply because the world around you and your family has gone mad. It's okay to be living in this culture because God knew it would be this way, and He placed you here with a job to do. This book exists simply to reinforce the sanity and truth that will already ring familiar in your soul, making you a better Christian witness in a wounded, confused world.

This book is not a statement that I have somehow figured it all out, and that I am an expert on the subject of raising chaste young men. I am an expert on exactly nothing. I have no credentials other than being the mother of eight children, six of them sons. In raising those sons, I have noticed that some things have worked for us and could probably work for others.

This book is not a guarantee against subsequent moral failures by me or my sons. There is no way to predict if my sons will continue to stay on the straight and narrow path. Virtue, otherwise known as moral excellence, is a habit that has to be cultivated; at the time of this writing, my boys are in the habit of the virtue of chastity. Free will, however, is a funny and fearsome thing. God gave us the precious gift of free will—without which we cannot *choose* to love and are left as merely robots or slaves—and our free will is the one thing He will not touch. It's ours alone, and until the moment of our death, we are free to choose good or evil. At any moment, my mature, older sons could choose to go off the rails, and there is also no guarantee that my younger sons, still in grade school and junior high, will use their free will wisely. However, even if they or I should fall, I believe that what is written here has value.

This book is not a scholarly work, nor a book of research, nor a deep philosophical or theological treatise. This book is the equivalent of one Catholic mom sitting down over a cup of tea with another mom, in my kitchen, to talk informally but quite seriously about navigating this culture with your boys' morality and chastity intact—and to give you the confidence you need to do just that.

So, what is this book? It's just a casual conversation between friends.

Let's get started . . . .

Chapter Two

The Basics

I lay down the foundational principles below with three assumptions: you love God, you serve God, and you teach your children to do the same.

In other words, I assume I am preaching to the mothers in the Catholic choir.

Read this well: Your children are not stupid. They know very well if you take your faith seriously or if you are picking and choosing which parts of the Faith or the moral law to obey and they will interpret that to mean that they can, too.

If you are picking and choosing, you have lost your moral authority to teach your children obedience to Christ, as your children can easily sniff out a lack of integrity, and if you have lost your moral authority with your children by dissenting from Church teaching, my advice here will be ineffective.

Now that we have established your love of God, faithfulness to the Magisterium, and acceptance of the entire Deposit of Faith, let's start with general, foundational principles that we can put into practice.

In looking back on over a quarter-century of parenting and asking my older children for their thoughts, I have identified three keys to raising solid, morally responsible kids in a culture of relativism:

1. Moral formation is the top priority.
2. What I teach must make sense.
3. Nothing is off limits for discussion.

Let's take them one at a time:

#1 Moral formation is the top priority

When I say "top priority," I mean that with every fiber of my being, and my kids know this. It really doesn't matter what else I do as a parent, because if I fail in the kids' moral formation and virtue training, I not only fail them, but I also fail society and God.

I have a suspicion that the average American parent no longer places "moral formation" at the top of his or her priority list. It seems to me that "academic/career/financial success" or "popularity" have taken the lead, followed by a general philosophy of "Whatever makes my child happy!"

Oy vey.

If we don't raise our children to be morally upright, first and foremost, then we miss the point of parenthood entirely. There are enough financially successful, popular, and "happy" villains in the world already. What we lack are *saints*! My children know—because I say it often enough—that I don't care if they are "happy." That's not my job. True happiness comes from the peace and joy of a life well lived. Lasting happiness is our goal—not temporary, giddy pleasures that cannot be sustained and that leave us bored, miserable, and looking for the next temporary high.

The virtuous, honorable man has a joy that no one can steal and a peace that surpasses all understanding, as Christ promised. That's what we are going for here, my friends. That's what we want for our children, and we mustn't be shy in telling them so. We want nothing less for them than eternal union with God in Heaven, which begins here on earth.

Now, it goes without saying that a child can be properly formed and still go wildly off the rails due to misuse of that pesky gift of free will. But woe to me if my child crashes into the ditch because I never placed and secured the rails in the first place.

#2 Our beliefs and principles need to make logical sense

Please understand this! We live in an age of nonstop information. Not knowledge, not wisdom—just information. All of these conflicting bits and chunks of data are competing with us for the very souls of our children. If we don't explain to our children why our Catholic Faith is logical, coherent, cohesive, consistent, and beautiful, they will have no reason to stick with it when the rest of the world tells them it's stupid, superstitious, oppressive, irrelevant, and evil.

Young people really do want to transcend the noise, chaos, and sin to find the straight path. They really do want their world to make sense, and our job is to show them that it does.

To that end, here is what we must never say to our inquisitive children:

"I have no idea why the Church is against [fill in the blank], or why we believe [fill in the blank]. You just need to follow the rules!"

No, no, no, no! What we say instead is:

"Well, Honey, I am not sure exactly why the Church teaches that, but I am going to find out and get right back to you. The Church always has a good answer."

That's when you open your *Catechism of the Catholic Church*, check reliable Catholic websites on the Internet (start with *Catholic Answers* at Catholic.com), or email me at Leila@LeilaMiller.net if all else fails. Resources to help you are everywhere.

I have watched the first five of my eight children reach adulthood. Each of the five has not only kept the Faith personally but also publicly. They have done so even in a hostile culture, while attending non-Catholic schools and large state universities, where the majority of their peers do not hold, understand, or even respect their Catholic worldview.

They have remained faithful through hardships and challenges because they see the truth of Christ's Church. It makes sense. It especially makes sense when contrasted with the literal nonsense and relativism that surrounds them. They are able to see in their non-believing, nonpracticing peers the consequences of living life in the "nonsense" versus living life as a faithful Catholic.

They certainly are not saints, and they have friends of all stripes and beliefs, but, by having the proper moral formation, they are able to make sense of the world, make sense of sin (their own and others'), and make sense of suffering. All the world, all of human activity, has a context for them, and *it makes sense*.

#3 Nothing is off limits for discussion

And I do mean *nothing*: sex, drugs, death, hell, crime, whatever. Age appropriate, of course, but nothing is forbidden.

My kids know that whatever they ask me will be answered. I am approachable, and I want them coming to me before they even think about going to anyone else.

A few years ago, my middle-schooler came to me with a one-two punch of shocking questions regarding things he had heard from his peers, things I could never repeat here. My face stayed relaxed, I met his gaze without betraying my alarm and horror, and I calmly gave him the explanations and information he needed.

When we finished our talk, he left the conversation relieved and satisfied, and so did I. The straight talk we had was informed by our Catholic faith, which *made sense to him* (principle No. 2), and the discussion was a catalyst for *deeper moral formation* (principle No. 1).

LEILA MILLER

See how seamlessly that works?

It sounds easy, doesn't it? And it is easy and uncomplicated—unless parents get caught in the starting gate, too spooked to go forward, specifically on the subject of sex. It troubles me when even devout Catholic parents say that they avoid such discussions or don't have them at all. They tell me they don't know what to say. I say, *too bad*. You have to do it. That's your job. They are your children, and you need to take them seriously, look them in the eye, and tell them the truth. They want to hear it from you, and they will absorb your wisdom on these matters. Don't let them down.

If you are still unsure if you can do it, it might motivate you to know that the Church herself is very clear on parents' *obligation* and *duty* to teach their children about sex. The Pontifical Council for the Family wrote an entire document on the subject in 1995: *The Truth and Meaning of Human Sexuality: Guidelines for Education within the Family*. I discovered this important document after a string of good Catholic mothers confessed to me that they could not or would not speak to their children (some already teens and adults) about sex. I was completely baffled, disturbed, and concerned. If these incredible Catholic moms weren't telling their children the truth about sex in a culture designed to destroy faith and devour souls, then who would? The answer, of course, is no one.

The Church calls parents to something higher than they might be aware. After I printed out the entire Vatican document, I took a yellow highlighter in hand and looked specifically for the words "obligation" and "duty." I was not disappointed by what I found. Here's a sampling (the following seven paragraphs are direct quotes; emphases in italics are in the original, and emphases in bold are mine):

In many cases parents have given up their **duty** in this field or agreed to delegate it to others, because of the difficulty and their own lack of preparation (No.1).

The Church has always affirmed that parents have the **duty** and the right to be the first and the principal educators of their children (No. 5).

Parents who carry out their own right and **duty** to form their children for chastity can be certain that they are helping them in turn to build stable and united families, thus anticipating, insofar as this is possible, the joys of paradise . . . (No. 33).

As husband and wife who have become "one flesh" through the bond of marriage, they share the **duty** to educate their children through willing collaboration nourished by vigorous mutual dialogue . . . (No. 37).

The Holy Father John Paul II reaffirms this in *Familiaris Consortio*: "The right and **duty** of parents to give education is essential, since it is connected with the transmission of human life; it is *original and primary* with regard to the educational role of others, on account of the uniqueness of the loving relationship between parents and children; and it is *irreplaceable and inalienable*, and therefore incapable of being entirely delegated to others or usurped by others," except in the case, as mentioned at the beginning, of physical or psychological impossibility (No. 41).

If in fact parents do not give adequate formation in chastity, they are failing in their precise **duty** (No. 44).

Parents in particular have the **duty** to let their children know about the mysteries of human life, be-cause the family "is, in fact, the best environment to accomplish the **obligation** of securing a gradual edu-cation in sexual life . . ." (No. 64).[2]

The Church understands and the document explicitly confirms that our duty as parents is more difficult today than it was in generations past. Why? Because before the sexual revolution and its corrosive effects on society and innocence, the greater culture—both secular and religious!—actually sup-ported families in the ideal, norm, and expectation of chastity. The document acknowledges that parents today cannot even rely on the past examples of parents and grandparents, as they did not have to face and counter what we parents have to face and counter today. Just like young men, we parents are also "battling the beast up close." This is a whole new ball game.

In addition to stressing parents' rights, responsibilities, and sacred duties, the Church stresses her own obligations:

> The Church holds that it is **her duty** to give parents back confidence in their own capabilities and help them to carry out their task (*The Truth and Meaning of Human Sexuality*, No. 47).

In other words, you are not alone! The Church is here to help, with an abundance of teachings, wisdom, reason, moral theology, and the power of the sacraments. Use what the Church is offering you as a parent. Christ established the Church to teach and sanctify the faithful on the journey through our earthly life and into eternity. Trust in the supernatural abundance of what she knows and what she can offer.

Now, let's get specific and practical. What type of parent/child relationship would make it easier to fulfill these sensitive and sometimes awkward duties?

I'm glad you asked . . . .

Chapter Three

Be His Parent And His Friend

We've all heard it: "Children need a parent, not a friend!" I had always agreed with this saying—had even repeated it loudly myself—and yet I began to wonder: Are parenting and friendship mutually exclusive? When I reflected on my own experiences as a mother, I concluded that they are not. I began to recognize that, like all human relationships, the parent-child relationship is deeper than any slogan.

I believe we can find a balance. I want to be, on an appropriate level, a true friend to my children. For years, I was embarrassed to admit that desire, fearful of being mistaken for one of the "cool" moms who make me cringe—the ones who are desperate for their kids to "like" them and who never quite grow up themselves. Clearly there is a danger in being too familiar with your child. Crossing the line into over-sharing, dumping your emotional baggage, or expecting a child to take on the role of an adult or partner is inappropriate and damaging. That kind of familiarity smacks of desperation, and the children of these needy and/or "cool" moms are often a mess themselves. Many eventually want very little to do with their mothers and have a hard time navigating their own relationships. Such familiarity is more an abdication of the parental role than a real friendship.

However, I want (and blessedly have) the kind of healthy, warm familiarity that finds even my high school sons home with the family on most weekend nights, piled onto our bed or sprawled out on the couch next to it as though they were still little kids. I don't mind their innocence and closeness. They are not strange, socially inept, or insecure—they just like hanging out with their parents and siblings, watching a movie or shooting the breeze on a Friday night. We've worked to cultivate that as parents, and I won't discourage it. Soon enough, as I know all too well, these moments will end, and they will be off to their adult lives. While the active parenting will be done then, the friendship will remain.

What kind of friendship between parent and child, then, is appropriate and desired? I like this definition of friendship that I found at CatholicCulture.org:

> Reciprocal love. In philosophical terms a friend is a person whom one knows and loves well and by whom one is known and loved for virtuous reasons. The biblical notion of friendship, in the New Testament, adds the feature of total selflessness after the example of Jesus Christ, whose love was generous, forgiving, and sought only the welfare of those whom he

loved. The sharing of confidences is also part of the biblical understanding of friendship (John 15:15).[3]

Friendship, then, is a special affection, a close relationship marked by enjoyment of each other's company, sharing things in common, having inside jokes, and a general feeling that "we like one another." True Christian friendship is grounded in a love of virtue, never a connivance in vice.

Parenting, which we discussed in the previous chapter, is the formation (character and moral) and education of one's children, requiring an exercise of God-given authority and a ton of confidence (fake it till you make it, ladies!). We are accountable before God Almighty for our parenting, which is our sacred vocational duty.

Maintaining a harmony between parenting and friendship is the challenge we face. Let's talk specifically about our sons.

My personal ideal, not always realized, is to be a firm and authoritative (not authoritarian) parent, and also a trustworthy, loyal, and cheerful friend. In my nonexpert, non-researched opinion based on personal trial and error, parenting and friendship can coexist, *so long as the parenting part stays firmly in place and takes priority if there is a conflict between the two.*

Strong, sound parenting helps facilitate a good friendship with your child. You cannot really have fun with and enjoy the company of a son whom you have not parented well. When a parent is loathe to firmly parent a child for fear of making the child "feel bad" or with the hope of sparing the child negative emotions, the child becomes ill-behaved, whiny, disobedient, entitled, manipulative, and overall unlikable! When I have allowed myself to be emotionally manipulated by a child, or when I didn't want to "hurt" him with boundaries and accountability, or when I was too lazy for follow-through my relationship with that child became strained, distant, and even hostile. Friendship at that point was impossible, as we really did not like one another. These were the hardest times in my parenting, as I think all moms can understand. We women are relational by nature, and it stings terribly when the mother-child relationship is wounded.

So, no matter how much you might dislike it, be a firm parent first and foremost. If you fear that your child will resent or hate you, consider the following story, which is one of the most gleeful memories I have:

My oldest son must have been about 12 years old, and he would readily admit that he was not an easy child to raise. He was in the swimming pool with some of the younger boys, and I was sitting outside watching. My son was on a tear of complaints, lamenting about whatever guideline or standard we were imposing on him, when he finally, nastily spat out the words: "You are the only mother I know who cares about her child's character!" What he thought would be a poison-laced dagger into my heart was in fact the cause of my instant joy! A huge smile broke out on my face, and I giddily responded with, "Yesssss! That is the best thing you could have ever said to me! Thank you for confirming that I am on the right track!" I danced around and laughed. Meanwhile, my son became mute and sulky, recognizing that he stepped right into that one, but I couldn't wipe the smile off my face for hours. Today, he and I are able to laugh about it, and he's glad that I was "that mom."

We want our children to understand that their character development and spiritual welfare are the most important things to us as parents, don't we? Isn't that the way they actually know that we love them?

Consider another incident, this time with my second son, which confirms that standing firm is exactly what our children want from us, despite what they say:

When he was a young teen, he had been manipulating me time and again about an issue. I wanted my boy to be "happy" and not mad at me, so I keep caving to his demands. This caving made him bolder and more obnoxious, until finally I'd had it. I put my foot down, asserted my authority, and yanked all his privileges. He knew I meant business. I'll never forget when that angry scowl turned into a gentle grin of approval, and he said, "Now that is some good parenting, Mom." Not sarcastic, not rude—the kid meant it! It was humbling to know that my previous attempts to placate him had actually been earning me his disrespect. He didn't like the consequences he now had, but he was actually thrilled that I was acting like a parent, not a pushover.

Which brings me back to the friendship part: It was only because we are friends that my son could be open and honest with me in saying what he did with a touch of humor. He didn't want me to fail in this endeavor of parenting, and because we are friends, he "had my number" and could call me on it. He encouraged me when I needed it. And when the proper order of authority was restored, the friendship rebounded as well.

You don't want to fall into the trap of being afraid of your children and their reactions when you lay down the law, but you don't want your children to be afraid of you, either. To that end, we must do what was not the norm in previous generations: We must apologize easily and openly admit our mistakes. Some parents go the other way and do not want to show any of their weaknesses, vulnerabilities, or humanity to their children. But then the parent becomes impenetrable to the child, and, frankly, unlovable. The lovability and affection between a mother and her son is crucial to parenting and formation, as it eases uncomfortable situations, facilitates tricky conversations, and makes it more likely that your child will really hear you when you speak and will come to you when he has a problem.

A while back, I had the following text exchange with my (then) 15-year-old son, which illustrates what can happen when a parent is also a friend. He came to me as a friend, and asked me, explicitly, to be a stronger parent:

"I'm gonna be honest. I'm not doing very well in French or chemistry."

"What does that mean? And how diligently are you studying?"

"That's the problem. I want to do well, but I'm too lazy. I need to be accounted for."

"Okay, then we need to do that, and you can't fight us. We are old and tired. But we can hold you accountable."

"I need that."

Boom! I'm going to count that as a parenting win, even indirectly. He made us more accountable in making him more accountable. Before we had a friendship, this particular son never would have confessed to bad grades on his own. The respect that's evident between parent and child in that text exchange might not have been there if the "friend" part of the equation had not been cultivated.

You might be thinking that if we had simply been harder on this child as he grew up, he would not be in this predicament. He has given me permission to share that we had an extremely difficult time with him for many years. In fact, we doubled-down on the "parenting" back then, neglecting the "friend" part for much of his young life. It was awful. We were awful. And there was no real affection, no trust, no enjoying each other's company.

We finally let go of the need for parental domination and control. We relaxed and remembered that he is beloved by and made in the image of his heavenly Father, and that no two children are the same. We began to enjoy his company and recognize his unique gifts. He came back "into the fold" of the family, and even found a more loving embrace from his siblings, who had also been put off by years of bad behavior. When the fighting lessened, everyone was happier and more relaxed. And yes, in backing off a bit, we let him experience the natural consequences of his own actions or inactions, part of which were poor grades.

When I was a younger mother, receiving that kind of text might have worried me or made me angry. As it stands, it didn't bring up any negative emotions toward my son. In reading his words, I sensed that this young man understood the need for the virtues of diligence and industriousness and was asking, on his own, for help to achieve it. The will was in place, an appropriate parent-child friendship was in place, and that's something we could work with!

Now that we've explored the general disposition needed to help us have that healthy relationship with our sons, in the next chapter let's get back to their formation in chastity and how that all begins . . . .

Chapter Four

When They Are Little

M ost of what you need to know about chastity and your sons' early years can be summed up in two sentences:

1. Respect the latency period.
2. Don't freak out about stuff.

The latency period, or what Saint John Paul II called the "years of innocence," spans from about age five to puberty and is easy enough to understand. From *The Truth and Meaning of Human Sexuality*:

> This period of tranquility and serenity must never be disturbed by unnecessary information about sex. During those years, before any physical sexual development is evident, it is normal for the child's interests to turn to other aspects of life. . . . So as not to disturb this important natural phase of growth, parents will recognize that prudent formation in chaste love during this period should be indirect, in preparation for puberty, when direct information will be necessary (No. 78).

Our Church tells us to respect the latency period of children, which would ideally last until the child hits adolescence; however, we live in a society that does not respect a child's innocence. In fact, the world around us seeks to destroy innocence by design. The educational establishment, advertisers, books, movies, television, and video games all push to sexualize children at a young age. Destructive entities such as SIECUS[4] and Planned Parenthood, which have routine access to public schools, believe that children should be immersed in secular, relativistic, "progressive" sex education from birth. The materials used for those even as young as kindergarten are sexually explicit and incredibly disturbing. Start an Internet search and see what I mean, but don't say I didn't warn you.

What's a parent to do when a child's latency period is violated? We must step in. Again, from the Church:

A further problem arises when children receive premature sex information from the mass media or from their peers who have been led astray or received premature sex education. In this case, parents will have to begin to give carefully limited sexual information, usually to correct immoral and erroneous information or to control obscene language (*The Truth and Meaning of Human Sexuality*, No. 84).

Dean and I have learned that precisely when to speak to our young children about sex, and how detailed to get, will be different for every child we have. For example, even as I sat down to write this chapter, I received the following text from the fourth-grade teachers at my son's public charter school:

"The birds and the bees seem to be of interest in the fourth grade! It has come to our attention that how babies are made is a topic of conversation. You may want to touch base with your child to see if he or she has been 'educated' by a peer."

And so, that very evening, my husband and I gently questioned our nine-year-old son to see if we had to "begin to give carefully limited sexual information" to him, as the Church directs. (Turns out, we did not.)

Another of our children, a daughter who was unusually precocious and curious, came to us with questions at the tender age of six. She was not satisfied with the usual, age-appropriate answers to "Where do babies come from?" and kept pushing, pushing, pushing ("But *how* does God make those babies?" "How does the baby *get* in the mommy's tummy?"). She was relentless, and so I finally gave her some basic biology—at which point she stopped asking, probably regretting her questions! I directed her not to discuss any of this with peers at her small, orthodox Catholic school, as I could just imagine the fallout from conscientious parents learning that their own little ones' latency periods had been disturbed prematurely! I myself was concerned by the whole situation, wondering if I had ruined my own daughter by telling too much too soon. I am grateful to report that this child, now a grown wife and mother, remained committed to her faith and to chastity, even after her early introduction to reproductive biology.

Another one of our children looked as if he might skate right on into adolescence itself without asking *any* questions, and so there came a day when Dean and I decided that he needed to hear from us before he heard from his peers. It was not so much disturbing his latency period as it was a prudential judgment that he was old enough and "in the world" enough to necessitate the discussion. We considered it a preemptive strike against what would have been a peer-driven, secular education had we not stepped in. In fact, we learned at about the same time that he had already begun to hear some talk about sex but had not let on that he did.

In our home, "the talk" consists of the same-sex parent (the boys with Dean, the girls with me) sitting down with the child and a book titled *The Joyful Mysteries of Life*—what we affectionately call "the little orange book." It's an unassuming, unadorned thin volume written by a French couple, Catherine and Bernard Scherrer, and translated into (sometimes awkward) English. The book contains an endorsement by Cardinal Alfonso López Trujillo, then the president of the Pontifical Council for the Family, who in his foreword describes it as an excellent companion to *The Truth and Meaning of Human Sexuality*. You would want to read through the book first in order to decide which (if any) parts to leave out.

At first I thought this little book would be too old-fashioned or hokey for today's more sophisticated kids, but I have been continually surprised by the positive responses we've gotten from the children. The last son who read it with Dean was our then fifth-grader, a "cool" kid who has it all together. Instead of making fun of the language and approach, this child would ask eagerly every night, "Is it time to read the next chapter yet, Dad?"

I wonder if we sometimes underestimate the power of the truth and how much our seemingly coolest, most independent sons want to hear about human sexuality from their parents, *not* their peers.

There are, unfortunately, two topics that will undoubtedly confront our children in some form or another before they have left the latency period: abortion and "LGBTQ" issues (homosexuality, "gay marriage," and transgenderism). These cultural tsunamis are so pervasive that they're going to come up, and they must be dealt with.

Explaining abortion to a young child is an awful, horrifying thing to do, and I hate it every single time. My kids start to hear the word "abortion" fairly young, as we are quite active in the pro-life movement. Prayers to end abortion abound in our parish, our kids' Catholic schools, and at the prayer vigils and Rosaries in front of local abortion clinics. At a certain point, I have to explain what abortion is.

Think about that. How does a mother explain abortion to her own child? But it must be done, gently and clearly. "Sometimes mommies or daddies don't want their babies and they pay a doctor to take the baby out too soon." Obviously, this is simplistic and not the full range of scenarios, but it's bad enough.

So far, every child has had the same reaction: disbelief, confusion, denial, and horror.

How could anyone do that? Who doesn't love little babies? Who forces a mom to do that? How could a mom ever do that to her baby? Why would a doctor do that?

They really get the evil of it. You don't have to paint a picture or get graphic. Children are naturally pro-life, and the idea of someone deliberately killing a child in his mother's womb is so foreign to small children as to be absurd, nonsensical, and insane. Their little minds sense the disorder immediately and reject it.

It does feel like I'm taking their innocence by telling them the terrible truth of it. After all, once a child understands that our nation not only allows but also celebrates the murder of other small children—the ones nestled in their mothers' wombs, just as they or their beloved siblings had been so recently nestled—how can they not be affected to their core?

After they experience that initial shock, don't forget to teach the mercy of God. Remind your child how much God loves all children and takes good care of the ones that have been lost in this way. And remind him to pray for the mommies, daddies, and doctors involved, that they might repent of this terrible sin, because God and those little babies want to see them all in Heaven one day. Explain how many people have changed their hearts on this issue and have gone on to become good men and women who fight against abortion now, similar to the way that Saint Paul used to help murder Christians but went on to become one of the greatest Christians of all!

More recently, "gay marriage," transgenderism, and "gender fluidity" have stormed onto the scene and have become unavoidable. What were not even issues when my first few children were born are now everywhere, even in children's programming. How can we explain all of this to them without going into details that they should not hear? Again: by keeping it simple. If a child comes to you and says that he's heard of people "changing" from male to female, or that he's seen two men kissing, you might just say, "Wow, they must be very confused! That's so sad. Let's pray for them so that they aren't confused anymore!"

Or, if they ask about two ladies being "married," you might simply say, "Nope, girls can't marry girls," just as we adults have responded for millennia when little ones innocently talk about marrying their friends or their same-sex parent. If an older child says, "But two men or two women are allowed to get married in America now," you simply remind the child that what is legal is not always right and that courts and judges can be—and often have been—horribly wrong. And as your child gets older, you will teach him about the truth and meaning of marriage (see Chapter Six).

Now let's get to the second point to remember when they are little: Don't freak out about stuff.

Catholic mothers tend to worry, worry, worry, even when we shouldn't. This worry is counterproductive. We worry about the safety of the world, the decline of the culture, the seemingly bleak future that awaits our children and grandchildren. For those macro worries, we must heed the words of Pope Benedict XVI, who reminds us that we were made for this time, and we are meant to be here on this planet, in this place, right now:

> Dear friends, may no adversity paralyze you. Be afraid neither of the world, nor of the future, nor of your weakness. The Lord has allowed you to live in this moment of history so that, by your faith, his name will continue to resound throughout the world (Homily, August 2011).

Mothers also worry about the little things. Every little thing, thousands of them—all the ways we could ruin our children or how they could ruin themselves. And yet, Jesus commands us not to worry, even in the micro, asking, "…can any of you by worrying add a single hour to your span of life?" (Mt 6:27). No, we cannot. Leave worry behind, and replace it with trust in God and His Providence.

Let's look at some specifics and get practical:

When a boy is a baby or toddler, he is likely going to touch himself and explore his genitals. This does not mean that he will become a compulsive masturbator, so relax. It's what little boys do. Boys like their penises. Some boys like their penises more than others, but you needn't be alarmed about it.

How do you handle it? Some boys only need to hear once or twice that "We don't play with our penis" or, cheerfully, "That's not a toy!" or my favorite as they get older: "Uh, that's not a handle!"—something I still say to my teens who routinely and unconsciously "adjust" themselves. It's become a bit of a joke, and I recommend a lighthearted attitude. Here's something I said to a youngster just before I typed this (and say often to all of them, who scratch and "reposition" no matter how old they get): "Get your hand out of your pants!" It's said firmly, but with a touch of good humor. They get it. And then I move along without dwelling on it or worrying about it. It's really not a big deal.[5]

In fact, little boy bits are so ubiquitous in our male-heavy home that even our kitchen table has not been safe from a brush with small genitals belonging to clamoring, climbing toddlers who would frequently present themselves naked to dinner! "Get your private parts off the table, please, and go get dressed!" We still laugh about it (and I'm guessing you all just made a mental note not to eat at our house).

Now, you may not agree with our earthy way of speaking and relating, and that's okay. I support parents' rights to direct and speak to their children as they feel called—and that might look more reverent or decorous in your home than in ours—as long as the necessary conversations are happening and innocent little boys are not shamed or made to feel dirty as they are being redirected. Whether you do your redirecting and virtue training with utmost reverence or with earthy good humor is your choice—as long as you do it.

By the way, I personally don't have a big emotional investment in whether or not other parents use proper, clinical words for their children's anatomy. Our kids know the technical names for their genitals, but we also call them "private parts" to get the "private" point across as well.

Now we are about to dive into a real irony. We Catholics do not want to have these difficult sex-related conversations with our small children in the first place. We want them to be children. We want them to keep their innocence and enjoy normal childhood relationships and development without everything being sexualized. And yet, it is Catholics who are accused, time and again, of being "obsessed with sex." Before we talk about adolescence and our teens, let's survey the cultural context and ground ourselves in the proper perspective . . . .

Chapter Five

The Two Big Accusations

Two charges are thrown against the Church so often and so reflexively that we must teach our children how to respond to them—and that means we must first know how to respond to them ourselves.

The First Charge:
"The Church Is Obsessed With Sex!"

If you speak to secularists at any length, or even to Christians who have wandered far from the virtue of chastity, you will hear the accusation constantly: "The Catholic Church is obsessed with sex!"

This silly charge is so pervasive and unquestioned that even many Catholics accept it as a given, and yet the claim is a head-scratcher to any reasonable observer, or to anyone who grew up Catholic in America.

I went to Mass every Sunday growing up in the 1970s and

'80s, and I don't recall ever hearing a homily about sex—not once. Today the topic might be more prevalent in some parishes due to the cultural shifts and crises, but even now it cannot even be said to be excessive, much less obsessive.

For those Catholics who make the claim that the Church is obsessed with sex, I'm guessing that they draw their views primarily or exclusively from media opinion, anti-Catholic teachers or professors, the entertainment industry, and/or secular friends—but certainly not from their experiences in a parish, a look at the *Catechism of the Catholic Church*, or an investigation into Church documents.

Anyone who's lived in both the secular world and the Catholic world (as I have, pre- and post-reversion) knows that it is the Church's accusers who are, in fact, obsessed with sex. It's actually wearying. Sex seems to be all they think about and want to talk about, and they command and coerce the rest of us to think about it and talk about it, too. All. day. long.

Can anyone plausibly deny it?

There is raunchy, ever-more-explicit TV and cable sex; ubiquitous, graphic movie sex; infinite hours of dark, depraved Internet porn sex; taxpayer-funded Planned Parenthood "sexperts" teaching our kids about oral sex, anal sex, group sex, masturbatory sex, homosexual sex, and making slick video tutorials for young people about the "skills needed" to navigate hookup sex; nonstop testimonials about the goodness of homosexual sex; dating sites for casual and adulterous sex; sex in commerce and advertising (can't they just sell us the burger?);

clothing that sexualizes little girls; explicit sexual lyrics in music; sex in music videos; simulated sex as dancing; sexting, sex tapes, girls and boys gone wild about sex, sex, sex, sex, sex! I even had commenters on my blog proclaim, quite seriously, that they COULD NOT LIVE without sex!

I think it's all a bit . . . *obsessive.*

And then we have the Catholic Church, plodding along through human history, saying the same thing about sex that she has always said. She is a teacher and a mother, and she is *responding* to the culture's errors, *reminding* an amnesiac world what sex and marriage are all about.

The Church, after all, has taught the truth about human sexuality and the virtue of chastity for over two thousand years, along with teaching the rest of the moral truths and virtues, which do not and will not change. Chastity just happens to be the virtue that today's sex-obsessed culture neither appreciates nor approves, but that's an indictment of the culture, not the virtue.

Marriage is a holy institution established by God, and sex—a privilege of marriage—is a one-flesh union of man and woman rooted in biology and ordered toward the good of the spouses, of the children created, and of society at large. Nothing new here—just the same ancient, beautiful, non-frantic, non-obsessive truth taught by the Church (sometimes even too timidly) for millennia.

Opposed to this timeless truth, the sexual "progressives" of our day are pushing a fad, working hard to fashion a new sexual paradigm where anything goes (between "consenting adults," of course!) and there are no moral judgments. The frenzied campaign is on, full-speed, to change our understanding of the very nature, meaning, and use of human sexuality. The Church's opponents want to redefine marriage and family to mean things they have never meant and can never mean, and they don't want anyone to tell them no. They are making incredible headway, and they are so close to their goal that they can taste it. But they remain frustrated. Something is keeping them from guilt-free, genital carte blanche.

The one thing standing in their way?

The Church. That's all. No generals, no armies—nothing. Just Holy Mother Church, speaking the same old truths she has spoken for 20 centuries and will speak for 20 centuries more, or until no one is left on earth to hear her. The Catholic Church is the one voice lovingly, carefully, firmly proclaiming—whether anyone listens or not—that sex has a meaning and purpose that cannot be discarded without violating our human dignity and the nature of love. Even when certain Catholics violate Church teaching on human sexuality, including clergy sworn to holiness, the evil fallout and devastation wreaked upon the innocent is not a *negation* of the moral law and the good of chastity but rather an excruciating *confirmation* of it.

Despite the utterly predictable, unwavering teachings of the Church, her opponents are often violently emotional in their quest to change her mind, silence her voice, or run her out of existence. Though they would like to claim an oppressor/victim model here, it's really more like a classic parent/teen showdown: "Give me my way and let me do what I want or I will scream at you and call you obscene names and tell you that you are power-hungry, irrelevant, out of touch, full of sin yourself, and just plain mean!"

And the Church, as a good mother does, looks on her children with love and concern—even sadness—but stays steadfast, consistent, and confident. The rules of life don't change. Truth does not change. Love does not change.

As the sex-obsessed voices get louder and angrier, the Church has tried to raise her voice above the din, but not because of any obsession. In fact, as far as I can tell, no one in the Church really enjoys constantly addressing the sexual morass in which we find ourselves (if only it would just go away!), but we have to speak loudly and clearly for the sake of a very confused generation. Because responding with love and truth to the prevailing sins of each age is pretty much the Church's job description, and it's what we can expect her to do from now until, well, eternity. That's not obsessive, it's just faithful.

All reasonable people can understand this, including teens. Each adolescent or teen sees the culture around him. He sees sex and porn and objectification shoved in his face every day from every angle. With his own experience of the culture and a correct understanding of the Church's role, fielding the "Church is obsessed with sex" question won't be the most difficult challenge your child will face.

The Second Charge:
"The Church Is Imposing Its Views!"

There is, however, another and more difficult accusation that will come to your children: "The Catholic Church has no right to impose its views on the world!"

The charge is so common now that most lukewarm Catholics accept it and many serious Catholics ignore it. But it's important that our children be able to see the landscape clearly so they aren't swayed by the sheer volume and frequency of the charge.

Let's get our bearings by making some distinctions.

On some issues, the left would be correct about "not imposing Catholic beliefs." Those issues and beliefs that we may not "impose" are the ones that are specifically Catholic.

If, for example, we Catholics were working to force people, by law, to attend Mass, to access the sacraments, to profess the Marian doctrines, or to abstain from meat on Fridays during Lent, our critics would be justified. We cannot impose points of the Creed, the unique tenets of our Catholic faith, on others.

But then there is the universal moral law, what is also called the natural law (not to be confused with physical science/"laws of nature"). The moral law is for all people, and all people are accountable to the moral law. These are issues of human flourishing, of virtue vs. vice, good acts vs. evil acts, and they apply to everyone in all times and cultures and places. These universal truths are accessible by the light of human reason alone (no divine revelation required).

Abortion, euthanasia, slavery, human reproductive trafficking, rape, murder, theft, lying, cheating, marriage as conjugal union, the primary rights of parents and the family—these things and more fall under the umbrella of the universal moral law, which is binding on all men.

Knowledge of the universality of the moral law is as old as mankind; pagans philosophized about it in ancient times, and it has undergirded every major world religion since. Our own nation's founding principles were predicated on a belief in natural law ("laws of nature and of nature's God" as the Declaration of Independence called it), and natural law was the basis of the Reverend Martin Luther King, Jr.'s arguments during the civil rights movement. He profoundly understood that the laws of men must correspond to God's law, as he explains in his famous "Letter from a Birmingham Jail" (1963):

> [T]here are two types of laws: just and unjust. I would be the first to advocate obeying just laws. One has not only a legal but a moral responsibility to obey just laws. Conversely, one has a moral responsibility to disobey unjust laws. I would agree with Saint Augustine that "an unjust law is no law at all."
>
> Now, what is the difference between the two? How does one determine whether a law is just or unjust? A just law is a man-made code that squares with the **moral law or the law of God**. An unjust law is a code that is out of harmony with the moral law. To put it in the terms of Saint Thomas Aquinas: an un-

just law is a human law that is not rooted in **eternal law and natural law** (emphases mine).

MLK understood what millennia of intellects, philosophers, statesmen, and saints have known but what our own recent generations have utterly forgotten. I myself had never explicitly heard of the natural law until I was in my early forties! Once it was explained to me, many things became clear.

If you are confused as to which topics are uniquely Catholic versus which topics are universal to all, there is a way to test it: You will find secularists and atheists who are against legal abortion (check *secularprolife.org*, for example), and you might even know some of them personally. You will also find secularists and atheists who believe in natural marriage—maybe your agnostic Uncle Al, or just check the atheist regimes around the world, whose heterosexual-only marriage laws obviously cannot be based on any religious tenets. What you will never find, however, are "Secularists for the Eucharist" or "Atheists for the Primacy of the Pope" or "Nonbelievers for Mandatory Baptism." In other words, you will find nonreligious folks everywhere who adhere to the moral law but none who adhere to the Nicene Creed.

Now, not every point of the moral law must or even should be enforced by civil law, but the biggies for humanity and society—such as human life itself, natural marriage, and rights of conscience—must be protected in law for the common good.

Still with me? Okay!

Let's go ahead and define our term. What does "impose"actually mean?

When searching the word "impose" online, this was the first definition that popped up, so let's use it for our discussion:

im·pose /im pōz/

verb

1 [To] Force (something unwelcome or unfamiliar) to be accepted or put in place.

Let's use "gay marriage" as our example here. If you followed the campaign for "gay marriage" in America and the massive, pull-out-all-the-stops push for its acceptance that culminated in a Supreme Court decision wiping out all state laws protecting natural marriage, something should immediately jump out at you when you evaluate the definition I just presented. Do you see it?

Just in case it's too obvious to see, let's break it down.

Marriage as union between male and female has been a reality (a non-controversy, a given) not only for the entire history of America but also essentially for the history of all mankind. I often refer to the *historically accurate* words of Hillary Clinton on the subject (shortly before her historical knowledge somehow "evolved" along with the political winds), when she stated her commitment to:

> ". . . the fundamental bedrock principle that [marriage] exists between a man and a woman, going back into the mists of history, as one of the founding foundational

institutions of history and humanity and civilization, and that its primary, principal role during those millennia has been the raising and socializing of children for the society in which they are to become adults."[6]

Bam! Yes, this!

Until about two minutes ago, historically speaking, this basic understanding of the inherent heterosexuality of marriage was the *status quo*.

A bride and a groom (sexual complementarity) are needed for a marriage = status quo.

Enter the "gay marriage" movement, with its advocates working very, very hard to change everyone's basic understanding of marriage. It's indisputable that the "gay marriage" movement was trying with all its might to change the forever-standing status quo.

When a movement or group comes in and labors to replace what exists with something new that it demands, that is called *imposition*. It's *imposing*. The "gay marriage" advocates (and not the Church!) have actually imposed their new view of marriage upon society.

Let's refer back to the definition above and plug in words to test it: The "gay marriage" movement has **forced (something unwelcome or unfamiliar) to be accepted or put in place**.

That fits.

And the force for acceptance has been powerful, as it was legally imposed from the top down. Meaning, the clamor and cry for the redefining of marriage did not grow upward from the American people as the 1960s-era civil rights movement did, but rather was instigated and pushed by secular elites, led by "progressive" lawyers, judges, professors, and politicians. Their aim was to displace society's status-quo (heterosexual) understanding of marriage, which had always been normal, comfortable, and quite acceptable to the people.

The truth is that all the movement, all the force, all the pressure, all the demands "to accept or put in place something unwelcome or unfamiliar" came from somewhere, but it was not from the Catholic Church.

Since our Catholic children are going to take a lot of heat if they stand for authentic marriage, let's take a closer look at the issue of "gay marriage," why it is not ontologically possible, and why acknowledgment of this truth is not simply a "Catholic thing". . . .

Chapter Six

The "LGBTQ" Juggernaut

When I first became a parent in the 1990s, I could never have imagined that one day I'd be raising children in a culture where "gay marriage" was put on par, legally or otherwise, with natural marriage, or where "gender fluidity"/transgenderism was seen as good, true, and healthy. And yet, now all of our children are living in a culture where they will have to make sense of what is around them, facing the questions and accusations of peers and even authority figures such as teachers and doctors.

It's important to recognize that gender identity politics has been forced upon us legally and socially in a fury. Just a few short years ago, much of what grips today's cultural conversation was unheard of, yet if we don't accept and embrace it, we are met with vile and rage-filled accusations, social shaming, and even legal punishment. The frenetic, urgent nature of it all, combined with the confusion, blurred lines, and disorientation it has brought, are hallmarks of the demonic. I say this not to strike fear or to be dramatic, but to help us better identify the underlying spiritual battle that this frenzied movement represents.

Consider that two things were present in the Garden of Eden with regard to human creation and relationships: 1) God created humans **male and female**, and 2) their relationship was a **marriage**. The devil, understandably, seeks to attack and destroy both of those realities.

"Gay Marriage"

Let's take the second one first. The "un-defining" of marriage has been going on for a while now: the acceptance of divorce stripped marriage of its *permanent* nature, and the acceptance of contraception stripped marriage of its *procreative* nature. With the acceptance of "gay marriage," the enemy's plan went into overdrive, stripping it of its *conjugal* nature. Let's tackle the most common objections to Catholic teaching on this issue by looking at the challenges your children are most likely to get.

Challenge 1:
"Why are you against gay marriage?"

It's not that we Catholics are against "gay marriage" per se; it's that "gay marriage" is an ontological impossibility. It's like asking why we are against square circles. Marriage has an essence, a meaning. It has always been a certain kind of union of persons, specifically a conjugal union rooted in biology itself; it is complementary and heterosexual by its very nature. The particulars of marriage contracts have varied over time and cultures, but the essence of male/female has not. Brides have always presupposed grooms.

The fact that marriage is what we might call a "universal" throughout human history indicates something huge—namely that we recognize this one particular type of personal relationship (male/female sexual union) as unique among all others. The reason should be obvious: It creates more humans. That children result from the union of man and woman (now father and mother) is the foundational reason that human societies have had a vested interest in protecting, elevating, and/or providing benefits for this type of union.

Without this sexual complementarity, and without the ability to have an actual union of bodies, there can be no marriage. With bodies of the same sex, the marital act physically cannot be completed; consummation is not possible. A bride implies a groom in the same way that a lock implies a key. Two locks make no sense together. Two keys make no sense together. The union of husband and wife, like the integration of lock and key, is a relationship different from any other.

Challenge 2:
"But what about heterosexual couples who are infertile? They are allowed to marry even though they can't procreate!"

The completed sexual union of male and female is always

ordered toward procreation, even if the couple does not actually conceive a child. Age, illness, or a medical disorder of
the reproductive system may render specific unions infertile,
but those things do not change the *nature* of the sex act itself,
which is *by its nature* generative. The conjugal union itself, and
not the fruit of that union, is the seal of the marriage. Produc-
ing children is not the basis of a valid marriage, the conjugal
union is. Whether or not children are conceived is beyond human control, and it's not the conception of children that makes
a marriage—it's the total, one-flesh union of husband and wife,
which is *by its nature* life-giving.

And as we've all known infertile couples who've eventually conceived years or even decades after their weddings, we
can never say with certainty who will or will not be childless.
God and nature have ways of surprising us. However, we can
say with complete certainty that two men will never conceive
a child from their sexual acts, nor will two women. *The sexual
"union" of two men or two women is always barren, as nature and
right order would have it.* That's not "unfair" any more than it's
unfair that the heart pumps blood or that my eyes are hazel.
That's simply the way it's supposed to be.

Challenge 3:
"What about men and women who are handicapped and not able to consummate? Are you saying that they cannot be married?"

This is a very delicate subject to discuss precisely *because* we have forgotten that marriage is a conjugal union. If there is no possibility of becoming "one flesh," not even one time, then the essence of marriage is missing. A relationship between two people without the ability to achieve sexual intercourse is called a friendship. That sounds cold to the modern ear, since we want everyone to feel good and "be happy," but feeling good at the expense of what is true can never satisfy, not ultimately. For marriage, one must be capable of performing the *marital act* (aptly named), at least one time.

Impotence or the inability to consummate is an impediment to the Sacrament of Matrimony for sure, but even the secular state will annul a civil marriage on the basis of non-consummation, which speaks to how universally and inherently humans understand the conjugal nature of marriage, whether civil or religious.

Now, with today's medical technology, thank God, there are many ways to treat or cure impotence and allow for marital relations. That is an incredible blessing.

Challenge 4:
"So you think marriage is all about sex! Can't you see it's about love?"

No, marriage is not "all about sex," of course—but sex is an intrinsic part of marriage. As mentioned above, a close and intimate relationship without sex is called a *friendship*, and neither church nor state would have reason to officially validate, elevate, or assign a special status to a friendship, as wonderful, important, and intimate as friendship is.

Also, while romantic feelings (what the culture calls "love") are ideal and desired between spouses, they've never been a prerequisite for valid marriage. To say they're required would be to deny that many of our own relatives and ancestors were actually married! My paternal grandparents, for example, did not know each other well when they became husband and wife. Yet they were married for over 50 years, raised five children while living in various war zones, immigrated to America, and have oodles of progeny. A particular feeling or emotion at the time of their wedding was not what made their marriage real.

Hey, if you ask Golde and Tevye (you all are huge *Fiddler on the Roof* fans like me, right?), they'd say their arranged-but-*consensual* marriage turned out just fine, even though they met on their wedding day. Yes, they are fictional characters, but they are representative of millions of valid marriages in the history of mankind. And we should note that their understanding of their love is closer to what authentic love actually is: a choice. A choice to serve and to will the highest good of the other, regardless of when or whether feelings of romance are present.

Challenge 5:
"But the state says that gay people can marry, so that means they can!"

There are many things the state has said that are legal fictions, i.e., that are not true or based in reality. For example, governments have declared at various times by law that certain human beings are less human than others (slaves, Jews, the unborn), or that women are men and men are women (transgender laws). None of those laws can change reality. The law is not magic, and it cannot make some humans less human, it cannot make men turn into women, and it cannot make marriage between two men (or two women) possible.

The state can manipulate words, but it cannot change essences. The manipulation of words can certainly wreak havoc, however, and we should be very wary when any political agenda bursts forth in a frenzy, seeking to sever a culturally primal word (human, man, woman, marriage) from anything it has meant before.

Basically, when someone says to me, "Look, if the state says two men are married, then they're married!" this is what I hear:

"Look, if the state says that cats can be dogs, then cats can be dogs!"

"Look, if the state says that a woman can be a man, then women can be men!"

"Look, if the state says that Jews are not human, then Jews aren't human!"

"Look, if the state says that black people can be the property of others, then they can be!"

"Look, if the state says that the unborn are not human beings, then they aren't!"

(Four out of five of those "truths" have happened, by the way.)

I teach my children not to lie. I will not go along with a lie. I will not teach my children to go along with a lie.

Marriage is pre-political; no state invented it, nor can any state redefine it. To illustrate how deeply this goes, consider the etymology (word origin) of the words "marry" and "matrimony"—they are derived from the word for *mother*, because marriage makes mothers! So, the meaning of the word "marriage" itself *excludes the very concept of a homosexual "marriage."* The very term "gay marriage" is self-refuting and self-negating. Even the word "groom" is shortened from "bridegroom"— wherein a groom presupposes a bride!

Of course, the government can assign specific public benefits and provide services to whomever it wishes (that's within its legitimate authority), but what it cannot do is redefine an institution that is based in nature itself.

Challenge 6:
"How does gay marriage affect you, anyway?"

Let's first compare that to another, similar question: "How does a woman's private decision to have an abortion affect you, anyway?" We can see that even if we are not "directly affected" by legal abortion (i.e., the one aborted or the one aborting), the entire culture is changed and reordered because of it; the "private" killing of millions has had a profound effect on the national psyche, and the lack of reverence for human life spreads systemically, like a pall, through our land.

Likewise, with the "gay marriage" question, the consequences for marriage, children, family, and society are numerous and far-reaching. Anytime a society "un-defines" its essential foundation (marriage is the first society), the corrupting effects hit everyone, without exception. First, there are the myriad legal attacks on religious freedom and conscience rights, which were not only the bedrock of this nation's founding but also sacred rights given to us by God.

However, if "gay marriage" and homosexual acts are "human rights," as we are now told, then opposing them in any way, even by politely declining to facilitate or participate in a same-sex "wedding," is seen as intolerable. Faithful Christians, including Catholics and the Catholic Church, thus become *discriminators under the law*,[7] with all the necessary legal punishments put in place for that offense.[8] Across the nation, Catholic foster and adoption agencies, and mom-and-pop businesses such as florists, bakers, printers, and photographers, have been forced to fight the unlimited power of the government and even close their doors due to lawsuits seeking to force them to violate their Christian beliefs.

Thankfully, since the first edition of this book was published, President Donald Trump has put in place a new division within the Department of Health and Human Services (HHS) that is dedicated to protecting conscience rights and religious freedom. But that protection is only as good as the next administration, when it easily could be stripped from us again.

Aside from lost liberty, the confusion that's been brought into the minds and hearts of the populace, especially our children, is devastating. It corrupts right thinking on the issues of marriage and family, obscuring what it's all *for*. If our laws and our culture say that a bride and a groom are no longer essential to marriage but that any sexual pairing (or more) will do, then fatherhood and motherhood themselves become meaningless to children—because generic "parent" is the only thing of cultural value that remains. In that case, children themselves become a commodity, as every type of "married couple" is seen as having a "right" to a child.

The Church in her wisdom speaks a truth that the culture does not want to hear:

A child is not something *owed* to one but is a *gift*. The "supreme gift of marriage" is a human person. A child may not be considered a piece of property, an idea to which an alleged "right to a child" would lead. In this area, only the child possesses genuine rights: the right "to be the fruit of the specific act of the conjugal love of his parents," and "the right to be respected as a person from the moment of his conception" (*Catechism of the Catholic Church*, No. 2378, emphases in original).

When children are denied their natural, God-given rights in favor of fabricated adult "rights" (based on desires, not truth and the created order), we undermine the very meaning and stability of family and society themselves. No sea change is without profound consequence, and so the question really should be: How does "gay marriage" *not* affect every one of us?

Challenge 7:
"You should be concerned about all the ways that heterosexuals have weakened marriage!"

I am incredibly concerned about that! Divorce (especially the pernicious "no-fault" divorce), adultery, polygamy, polyamory, premarital sex, hookups, contraception, abortion, etc.—all of that has gravely harmed the institution of marriage and, as always, children. But just because we've severely damaged marriage, that's no argument for demolishing it completely, is it? The proper response to the sad state of marriage today is to strengthen it, not to un-define it into oblivion.

Besides, every heterosexual marriage that is weak, irregular, or even broken has at least the *potential* to be strengthened, regularized, and restored. But with two men (or two women), there is no potential for marriage in the first place (see Challenge 1).

I'll finish with this: While people often proclaim that there is no difference between traditional marriage and "gay marriage"—because "love wins" and "love is love" and all that—they know that it's actually not true. In fact, the essential mark of marriage, its intrinsic nature, must be cast off or put aside under the new paradigm. I saw this illustrated starkly when I came across the UK legal guidelines, intended

for the public's information, on "How to Annul a Marriage."[9]
I skimmed through the easy-to-read list of all the usual im-
pediments that would warrant a civil annulment, and then I
got to **consummation**, i.e., sexual intercourse, the one-flesh
union that seals the marriage bond. A legal marriage, it states,
is "defective" or "voidable" if it was never consummated (yep,
sounds right)—but then comes the elephant-in-the-room
caveat, placed parenthetically: "**(doesn't apply for same-sex
couples)**."

Blink. Blink.

So, consummation is an assumed, inherent part of all marriage—except for "gay marriage." Why? Because a same-sex
couple cannot consummate a marriage, not ever. Gay couples
cannot achieve sexual union, they can only simulate it. The UK
government knows this, and deep down we all know this. Even
a young gay friend of mine, who was "married" to his boyfriend (then quickly divorced), agrees with me privately (it's
not something he can say publicly) that same-sex "marriage" is,
in his words, an "**imitation** of heterosexual marriage." And yet
the pretense goes on.

If even the civil law has to specify two different sets of rules
for what we are told is "the same thing," then those two things
are not actually "the same," are they?

This is the kind of reasoning our children must understand
and be able to articulate in order to stay firm in their faith and
in chastity.

The Transgender Movement

Back to the Garden.

Now that God's created relationship between man and woman—namely, marriage—has been unraveled and dispensed with, it's time for the enemy to obliterate "male and female" creation itself. It's no accident that immediately after the legalization of "gay marriage," the issues of transgenderism and "gender fluidity" zoomed to the forefront of our cultural consciousness, furiously demanding our acceptance, or else.

This is where things get a little spooky, because it's one thing to convince folks to accept that attributes of a relationship (marriage) can change, but quite another to convince them that what is biologically, actually real is not real (e.g., this man is not a man, but a woman).

To help a child understand the simple truth of "being," go to the Internet and show them the ad that was created by CNN in October 2017 to address "fake news" accusations. The same network that has no problem at all with calling men "women" and vice versa (and using female pronouns for folks like Bruce/Caitlyn Jenner) created a "Facts First" ad that is instructive and unintentionally ironic. Using a simple picture of an apple—something we recognize as a knowable thing, one that can be scientifically verified if anyone doubts it—they say: "This is an apple. . . . Some people might try to tell you that it's a banana. They might scream *banana, banana, banana*, over and over again. . . . You might even start to believe that this is a banana. But it's not. This is an apple."

The makers of the ad are 100 percent correct. And if they can get it so right on the truth that an apple is an apple (no matter what others might demand that it is or demand that we call it), then why can't they understand that a man is a man and not a *woman, woman, woman*? Of course, the answer is secular "progressive" ideology and identity politics, which are fiercely anti-Catholic and which blind even intelligent people to the obvious truth.

Because you don't want your children to fall prey to this ideology, it is imperative that you teach them from a very early age how to rightly reason. If they get to the teen years having based their ideas and worldview on feelings rather than truth, it's harder to bring them back to reality. I strongly urge a return to fables and morality tales for our children, and, in this day and age, the most important fable to repeat, even to the point of memorization, is *The Emperor's New Clothes*. Simple things like that tale, or even the CNN ad, are tools we can use to form and protect our kids' thought processes before the culture gets ahold of them.

The devil hates God and God's human creation, so it's no wonder he is aggressively targeting marriage and our very essence as male or female. Thankfully, we see his evil plan,[10] and with God's help and grace, we can foil it before it distorts our children's minds and hearts.

Now that we are clear-thinking on marriage and the sexes, let's tackle what chastity looks like for a young man, before and after marriage . . . .

Chapter Seven

Chastity Before And After Marriage

Q uick disclaimer: The truth and beauty of human sexuality and the virtue of chastity, as presented by Saint John
Paul II in his earth-shattering teaching on the Theology of the
Body (TOB), is far beyond the scope and purpose of this book,
much less this chapter. As a parent and simply as a Christian,
you really must become familiar with TOB. To that end, I have
included resources in the Appendix.

In this chapter, I offer only a snapshot of what chastity
before and after marriage looks like so that the very basics will
make sense to your son.

An astoundingly common mistake—and one that I made
for years—is to think of chastity and abstinence as synonyms.
They are not. Sexual abstinence means refraining from sex,
whereas chastity is a lifelong virtue to which we are all called
in every state of life, including the married life. If that sounds
confusing, let's look at how the Church defines chastity and go
from there:

Chastity means **the successful integration of sexuality within the person** and thus the inner unity of man in his bodily and spiritual being. Sexuality, in which man's belonging to the bodily and biological world is expressed, becomes personal and truly human when it is integrated into the relationship of one person to another, in the complete and lifelong mutual gift of a man and a woman (*Catechism*, No. 2337) (emphasis mine).

In other words, to be chaste is to live with sexual integrity. Sex is a privilege of marriage, so in order to maintain bodily and spiritual integrity, an unmarried person lives out chastity by refraining from sexual activity. This means: no sexual intercourse, no oral sex, no heavy petting, no touching or stimulation of one's own or others' genitals.

The self-mastery required for premarital chastity is not always easy, but it's always worth it. Because the marital embrace is the complete gift of self, body and soul, to one's spouse, chastity before marriage preserves the gift while also preparing the man to be a good husband. From Catholic writer and professor Mark Lowery:

You cannot have a healthy marriage without chastity—that virtue by which we are in control of our sexual appetite rather than it being in control of us. And chastity is a tough virtue to develop. If it is not in full development before marriage, it is going to be very hard to develop after marriage. So, before marriage is the time to accomplish this very positive thing, the virtue of chastity.

This is a courageous thing to do, a positive thing to do. **Males need to see it as the ultimate manly thing to do,** and they need to take the lead in the couple's mutual accomplishment of moral toughness (emphasis mine).[11]

Arleen Spenceley, a staff writer for the *Tampa Bay Times*, sums it up beautifully:

Abstinence just challenges us not to have sex. Chastity challenges us to live lives in which desire is subservient to reason, which equips us to love as Jesus does: selflessly.[12]

If our sons know to prepare well for sports competitions, major exams, and future careers, but are not preparing well for marriage—or for the priesthood, which is a spiritual marriage—then they have missed the key training, the one that will sanctify them and bless future generations.

After the solemn marriage vows have been exchanged in the presence of God and His Church, chastity includes sexual union and is lived out freely, totally, faithfully, and fruitfully. There is nothing held back, no part of husband and wife withheld from each other, body or soul, including the astounding gift of fertility—just as God designed it.

Because we in the western world have been so thoroughly indoctrinated with the idea that contraception even for married couples is the "responsible" thing, and because even Catholic kids might shrug off contraceptive use as "no big deal," we must reorient our thinking and theirs. Our sons will naturally understand why adultery, porn, and spousal rape offend against chastity in marriage, but they may not fully understand why contraception offends as well, so that's where my focus will be. Please remember the principle we talked about earlier, that *things must make sense to your child* if you expect him to stand strong against the errors of the day.

Your children possess reason, and they can see that every created thing has a specific *nature* and *design*. When a thing is used according to its nature and design, it's being used correctly and will yield the very best of results. However, when we misuse a thing, or derail its design, we get into trouble. This is common sense, and even a small child can understand it. (Ask your small child if a spaghetti noodle makes a good sewing needle!)

So, if we're going to say that contraception is a positive good, then we also have to say that God's original design for sex and for our bodies was wrong, or at least was lacking something important. There's no way around it.

But let's think: When God was creating human beings, did He somehow "forget" that we needed contraception? Did He overlook or not understand that humans want to have sex without making children from that act? Did He accidentally connect pleasurable sexual union with procreation? Did the

Creator mess up so badly that we creatures needed to come in and add what He'd forgotten or fix the plan He botched?

Judging from the number of times I've heard Christians say, "God gave us the brains to invent contraception," one might conclude that people *do* believe that condoms, diaphragms, spermicides, pills, patches, rings, sponges, caps, implants, shields, injections, IUDs—and whatever other contraceptives I am forgetting—were a necessary improvement on God's first defective attempt.

However, when we talk about our fertility, we are not talking about a disorder, defect, or disease of the body that needs treatment or fixing (such as when a failing heart needs medication, poor eyesight is corrected with lenses, a ruptured organ is repaired in surgery, or a missing limb is replaced by a prosthetic). Instead, we are talking about God's own design for the body, which, when working properly, is called "health." It is the *healthy* operation of a bodily system that contraception seeks to derail.

Of course it's silly to think that an all-knowing, all-powerful, all-good God made any mistake at all, much less a mistake involving the very mechanism He chose to bring eternal human beings into existence. Obviously, God designed our bodies, our reproductive systems, and marriage exactly as He wanted. It is our "addition" of contraception (and our acceptance of surgical sterilization) that is the mistake.

While it is true that various forms of contraception have been around since antiquity (as have abortion, adultery, fornication, masturbation, and a host of other sins connected to human sexuality), Christians have always condemned its use as gravely sinful. We've become so disconnected even from recent history that it's necessary to look back at just how the widespread acceptance of contraception came to us—and how abortion came right on its heels, as the deadly fruit of a rotten tree.

On the secular front, eugenicist and atheist Margaret Sanger spearheaded the birth control movement with her 1921 founding of the American Birth Control League, now known as Planned Parenthood. Although Sanger herself did not champion abortion, she labored for contraception under the slogan "no gods, no masters"—a clarion, overt rejection of Christianity if there ever was one!

On the Christian front, the acceptance of contraception began with the Anglican Church in 1930, when it cracked the door to allow contraception *only* for married couples, and only in serious situations—the "hard cases." By the following year, an association of Protestant denominations, the Federal Council of Churches, approved married couples' "careful and restrained use" of contraceptives.

It's important to note that at the time the birth control movement began, secular and religious sentiment had been largely in harmony regarding the evils of contraception (as happens with natural law issues), and so condemnatory responses came from both camps.

The secular *Washington Post* editorial board wrote the following in a 1931 editorial, after the Federal Council of

Churches endorsed the Anglicans' 1930 Lambeth Conference condoning limited artificial birth control use:

> It is impossible to reconcile the doctrine of the divine institution of marriage with any modernistic plan for the mechanical regulation of or suppression of human life. The Church must either reject the plain teachings of the Bible or reject schemes for the "scientific" production of human souls.
>
> Carried to its logical conclusion, the committee's report, if carried into effect, would sound the death knell of marriage as a holy institution by establishing degrading practices which would encourage indiscriminate immorality. The suggestion that the use of legalized contraceptives would be "careful and restrained" is preposterous. (March 22, 1931)

And Father Fulton Sheen, not yet a bishop, weighed in with his own prophetic assessment: "Since a week ago last Saturday we can no longer expect them to defend the law of God. These [Protestant] sects will work out the very logic of their ways and in 50 or 100 years there will be only the Church and paganism. We will be left to fight the battle alone—and we will."[13]

Many Protestant denominations were outraged by the Federal Council of Church's deviation from Christian moral teaching and put out statements of denouncement. However, within a few years, they all caved. Today, contraception as a positive good and a responsible choice is taught by all major

Protestant denominations, with nary a reflection. Most Americans don't remember it being any other way.

By the 1960s, the hormonal birth control pill was all the rage, and it was touted as a boon and blessing to women, marriage, and family. Everything was going to be better now, the people were told. Even the Vatican's birth control commission, set up to study the question of contraceptive use and population issues, made a case that artificial birth control should be allowed. But in 1968, Pope Paul VI rejected that recommendation and instead reiterated the unbroken teaching of the Church in his landmark encyclical *Humanae Vitae*.[14]

Upon its release, the pope's document was met with disbelief, dismay, fury, mass disobedience, and widespread dissent, even on the part of countless clergy and, shamefully, bishops. Yet the encyclical's prophesies have all been borne out, including the following, which we see all around us today:

> [Contraceptive use will] open wide the way for marital infidelity and a general lowering of moral standards. Not much experience is needed to be fully aware of human weakness and to understand that human beings—and especially the young, who are so exposed to temptation—need incentives to keep the moral law, and it is an evil thing to make it easy for them to break that law. Another effect that gives cause for alarm is that a man who grows accustomed to the use of contraceptive methods may forget the reverence due to a woman, and, disregarding her physical and

emotional equilibrium, reduce her to being a mere instrument for the satisfaction of his own desires, no longer considering her as his partner whom he should surround with care and affection (No. 17).

The love in these words, the care of Holy Mother Church for the bodies and souls of her children, is so evident here! Yet, this love was rebuffed along with the truth, and the rebellion raged in earnest.

As the law of natural consequences would have it, the acceptance of contraception swiftly led to the acceptance of abortion.

For example, Planned Parenthood went from peddling contraception to peddling abortion, and today it is the largest provider of abortion in our nation. The progression from contraception to abortion was natural and easy.

Similarly, many of the Protestant denominations that accepted contraception are now fully on board with abortion today. The Episcopal Church (the American branch of the Anglican Church that first permitted contraception) now officially and proudly supports abortion rights, as do several other mainline Protestant denominations. For much of Protestant Christianity, the progression from contraception to abortion has been natural (if not always easy).

Now let's look at how abortion came to us legally in America.

Roe v. Wade was the 1973 Supreme Court decision that legalized abortion nationwide, and a "right to privacy" legal argument was used as the basis for that tragic decision. However, most Americans are unaware that the "right to privacy" (words not found in the Constitution) did not originate with *Roe v. Wade*, but with *Griswold v. Connecticut* in 1965 and *Eisenstadt v. Baird* in 1972. What were those cases? Griswold was the case that legalized the sale of contraception to married people, and Eisenstadt was the case that extended the same "right" to unmarried people. The "right to privacy" regarding contraception cleared the way for the "right to privacy" regarding abortion. The legal road from contraception to abortion was natural and easy.

Even the liberal justices on the Supreme Court of the United States (*Planned Parenthood v. Casey*, 1992) understood clearly that contraception is a social contract that says, in essence, "We agree to have sex but we do not agree to have a baby." Because contraception fails so often, the contract needs a fool-proof backup, and that backup is abortion. The Court, reaffirming legal abortion, put it this way:

> . . . for two decades of economic and social developments, people have organized intimate relationships and made choices that define their views of themselves and their places in society, **in reliance on the availability of abortion in the event that contraception should fail**. The ability of women to participate equally in the economic and social life of the nation has been facilitated by their ability to control their reproductive lives (emphasis mine).[15]

We should sit up and take notice when the pro-abortion

members of the Supreme Court *and* the Catholic Church see the same truth. Though on opposing sides of the abortion issue, both entities understand that contraception and abortion are symbiotically connected. How do they see so clearly what most Christians do not?

God's providence never fails us, of course, and each time sin and error ramps up, grace abounds even more: At the precise moment in history that the pill stormed onto the scene, science was giving us ever-expanding knowledge of human fertility. Faithful Catholics who had just reasons to postpone pregnancy went from using the largely unreliable calendar method ("rhythm method") to the highly scientific and accurate methods of natural family planning (NFP).

NFP and fertility awareness, which is permitted and promoted by the Church, is essentially *information* about how our bodies and our fertility work. This scientific information can be used not only to postpone a pregnancy but also to achieve a pregnancy, to help overcome infertility, and even to assist women and girls suffering from menstrual disorders. NFP always respects and works *with* God's design, and, unlike contraception, it does not in any way change the nature of the marital act. It is completely compatible with the virtue of chastity.

Like TOB, NFP is a huge topic with many facets and, therefore, is beyond the scope of this book. However, I've included resources in the Appendix, including a link explaining why using NFP to avoid pregnancy is most definitely *not* "just another form of contraception."

By the way, all of the teenagers in the Miller house, both boys and girls, are presented with a solid overview of the science of NFP so that they understand long before marriage how incredibly ordered our bodies are. They know that we are "fearfully and wonderfully made" by the Lord, and that the gift and blessing of fertility is to be revered, not reviled.

In the next chapter we'll look at another common enemy of chastity that has gained widespread cultural approval, and it's one of the biggest snares your boys will face . . . .

Chapter Eight

Straight Talk About Masturbation

Never in my life did I envision writing an entire book chapter on masturbation, and I'm guessing it's not a topic that most of you would generally choose to read about. When I sat down to write this, I told the folks on my Facebook page about the subject matter, and the one-liners and double entendres that came forth (nothing vulgar, just some levity) were pretty amusing.

Indeed, the subject of masturbation is the fodder for many clever jokes and puns, but what really struck me is that while most of the jokers were faithful Catholics, one of my more secular friends responded to the topic of masturbation with a simple "Ick." That kind of sums it up, doesn't it?

It's an icky subject, and despite the "enlightened" talk of "healthy" masturbation—even by some Christian leaders who should know better—masturbation is an inherently shameful activity, and on some level we all know it.

If you doubt that, then consider: We do not hear people

proudly and openly discussing their prowess and expertise with masturbation. They may admit that they do it, they may even talk about it, but no one aspires to be the best at it. No one talks of how he has perfected his masturbatory techniques, and no one brags about high frequency: "I am the most expert masturbator there is! I masturbate more than anyone I know, and I am incredibly proficient at it! I'm what you'd call the master of masturbation!" Um, ewww. This is no way to attract the ladies, and even the guys in the locker room will likely keep a safe distance from the dude touting his special "talent."

By contrast, millions of men boast of their sexual prowess *with others*, both quality and quantity. We see this all around us, every day. We grew up hearing the "players" in high school and college discussing and embellishing their sex lives with pride. We also have movie and television stars, musicians, social media celebs, sports heroes, and corporate tycoons, many of whom would be thrilled to be known for their sexual "accomplishments" and abilities, and hopeful for the press to advance that image.

Now, when men crow openly about prolific sexcapades with others, their hearers may either stand in admiring awe or scowl with disapproval, but they will not instinctively, viscerally cringe as they would at a loud and proud masturbator. Let's face it: Sex with a partner is one thing (even if sinful), but having "sex" with oneself is quite another.

Again, let's think about our human nature and how we were made by God. Each male and each female has exactly *one half* of a reproductive system. In fact, the reproductive system is the only system of the human body that is completed by someone else! Picture a male or female body in isolation, and it does not make any sense without the body of the opposite sex to complete the picture. The truth that the sexual faculty was made for *other* and not *self* is not some complicated, esoteric riddle to decipher. It is plain. Sexual complementarity is written right into the design of our very bodies.

Every system of the body has a design and a right order for use. Here's a rough analogy to the eating faculties: The glutton often has no shame eating copious amounts from the banquet table. In fact, like the sexual conquistador, he may celebrate and publicize his accomplishments and proclivities. He is doing something that the body is naturally ordered to do, i.e., eat and drink, but he's taking that good thing to excess for pleasure's sake and forgetting its inherent meaning, i.e., nourishing the body.

But the bulimic, unlike the simple glutton, does his deed in secret. He is ashamed to expose his habit to others and would never brag about how often and expertly he abuses his own body by making himself throw up. The healthy body is not ordered toward self-induced vomiting. It's not how we are made, it goes against our nature, and it's a misuse of the digestive system. Just as with the masturbator, the bulimic has an intrinsic shame in misusing a bodily system by manipulating its functions to go *against the natural order*. In fact, we literally call bulimia a *disorder* for that reason.

I want to be very clear about something here, because the secular world is quick to misunderstand or misuse the word "shame." Shame can be felt inherently from within, and shame can be imposed on us from without. If I were to find out that my child was masturbating, I would not think of "shaming" that child. The act itself is inherently shameful and needs no more shaming from me. While I might indeed tell a child "shame on you" for proudly and *unashamedly* hitting his sister on the head with a frying pan (same goes for an older adolescent who started using girls for his pleasure), I would never "double shame" someone for an act, namely masturbation, that is already naturally embarrassing or shameful.

Okay, so the reproductive organs and sexual faculties are by nature ordered toward *other*. Because human beings are body *and* soul—integrated—the human person flourishes when his intellect and his will are in tune with the truth of his body. We can convince ourselves to ignore and act contrary to our very nature (we do this all the time, to our detriment, and it's called sin), but somewhere inside, we know the truth.

That is why even populations that have been taught and believed the complete "healthiness" of masturbation have, to their own surprise, found freedom and restoration in giving it up.

Consider that a few years ago on Reddit (the wildly popular social news and networking site that gets hundreds of millions of hits a month), the "NoFap" community was born. No-Fap is essentially a support group for those who take up the challenge to stop masturbating (and give up porn, its natural companion).

The group has tens of thousands of members, and though it is quite specifically not religious or moralistic in nature, it has led to a kind of redemption. As you can read for yourself on the "Ultimate Benefits"[16] thread, the fruit of living free from masturbation has led these men to wholly unexpected gains, including but not limited to:

- More confidence
- More control over all aspects of life
- Feeling more like a man
- Not as annoyed at others
- Feeling more respect from others
- Better relationships with women
- Better memory and clearer thoughts
- Better social skills
- More motivated and productive
- Better marriages (for married men)
- Feeling more positive
- Loss of mental fog
- Lifting of depression
- Feeling "alive"
- Clearer skin and deeper voice (I know! But these were reported by numerous men!)

It should not surprise any Catholic that there are benefits to not masturbating. We Catholics understand that by living virtuously and according to our nature, human beings, human relationships, and human societies flourish. We know that having self-control and integrity of body and mind is the key to interior peace and joy, and that if our intellect does not control our will, we are not truly free. The folks on NoFap may not understand that explicitly, but implicitly, they are living it—and reaping the benefits of increased sexual and relational health, without even knowing (yet) that it's the beginning of a spiritual triumph as well. For now, they are simply surprised and utterly delighted to find that the world without masturbation is a brighter, freer, more beautiful place!

A huge point I want to make about masturbation, and one that you must tell your sons, is that *not everyone is doing it*! We and our sons would not know this if we listened to the voices around us. The general sentiment of the culture can be summed up in the words of Dr. Joycelyn Elders, U.S. Surgeon General under President Bill Clinton, who said: "We know that more than 70 to 80 percent of women masturbate, and 90 percent of men masturbate, and the rest lie."[17]

Of course this is ridiculous (and frankly, insulting), and it's simply an attempt to normalize self-indulgence. One question I love to ask my boys when they are young is, "Who is the strongest man in the world?" Once we get past the excited, shouted responses of "God!" (no, I mean human man) and "Jesus!" (no, I mean mere mortal, created man) and "Superman!" (no, not pretend men like superheroes), I give them the real answer: "The strongest man in the world is the one with the most self-control!" This answer delights a boy's imagination, as he sees the sheer manliness of self-mastery in all areas. If a man can be strong and disciplined enough to become a star athlete, a concert-level musician, or a top scholar, he can certainly be disciplined enough to leave his private parts alone.

The Church is clear about the gravity of the sin of masturbation:

> By masturbation is to be understood the deliberate stimulation of the genital organs in order to derive sexual pleasure. "Both the Magisterium of the Church, in the course of a constant tradition, and the moral sense of the faithful have been in no doubt and have firmly maintained that masturbation is an intrinsically and gravely disordered action." "The deliberate use of the sexual faculty, for whatever reason, outside of marriage is essentially contrary to its purpose." For here sexual pleasure is sought outside of "the sexual relationship which is demanded by the moral order and in which the total meaning of mutual self-giving and human procreation in the context of true love is achieved" (*Catechism*, No. 2352).

Yet the Church also understands the conditions that afflict and weaken a person's resistance to the sin:

> To form an equitable judgment about the subjects' moral responsibility and to guide pastoral action, one must take into account the affective immaturity, force

of acquired habit, conditions of anxiety or other psychological or social factors that lessen, if not even reduce to a minimum, moral culpability (*Catechism*, No. 2352).

So, while we must recognize that masturbation is intrinsically immoral, we must remember that anxiety, habit, and immaturity can lessen culpability. But even with lessened culpability, the sad consequences remain: An immature teen with anxiety who habitually masturbates will not find maturity, confidence, and social/relational health until he leaves this particularly addictive sin behind.

An important note here about scrupulosity. If you believe your son suffers from scrupulosity—a fear of sin that puts him in a state of debilitating anxiety—drop everything and get him help. An overly scrupulous conscience is a serious hindrance not only to spiritual growth but also to daily functioning. Scrupulosity is a torturous psychological condition that we understand now to be one type of obsessive compulsive disorder (OCD). Scrupulosity affects people of all religions (and no religion), but a Catholic with this condition may obsess over blasphemous thoughts that invade his mind against his will; he may agonize about whether or not something he's done is sinful, even when other faithful Catholics and his priest have assured him that it's not; he may have a conscience so hypersensitive that he cannot find peace with God; and he may fall into deep despair when he does sin. To help your child or anyone suffering with the hell that is scrupulosity, please refer to the Appendix for resources and help.

Ultimately, we do our boys and young men no service by pretending that just a little bit of sexual sin now and then will not harm them, will not distort their view of themselves and women, and will not quickly become addictive in this age of ubiquitous porn. For parents not in the habit of conversing frankly about sex with their children, masturbation can be a difficult subject to broach—but just think how much more difficult things would be if you don't tell him and he becomes a compulsive masturbator who cannot become free.

That is a fearful thought, isn't it? Let's talk more about the place of fear in parenting . . . .

Chapter Nine

Fear Has A Place

Yes, fear has a place, and as a big proponent of "be not afraid," I don't mean that one should live in fear. Not at all! But a *healthy* fear of sin and hell is a good thing, especially in the nascent moral life. A proportionate, well-ordered fear of consequences can help keep our boys on the narrow path.

Before we are fully morally developed, don't we avoid certain acts out of a reasonable fear of natural consequences? We teach toddlers not to touch a hot stove for fear of getting burned. We teach non-swimmers not to jump into the deep end of the pool for fear of drowning. We teach teenagers not to speed for fear of getting a ticket or crashing the car.

If a boy sees no negative consequence for a given act, or if there is no explicated downside to a sin that feels good, then why avoid that act or sin? In fact, that is exactly what the world is telling your sons—that there is no reason to hold back on their sexual urges as long as the sex is "safe" (masturbation! condoms!) and "consensual" (get a "yes" from your partner and then anything goes!).

When one is a young, healthy male, acting on sexual urges can seem like a great idea. Many teens and young men do act impulsively, forgetting—or never having learned—that a thing as powerful as sex has to have limits, context, and meaning. Teaching your children about human sexuality is your parental obligation, as we've already discussed in Chapter One, and raising a young male with no fear of sexual consequences is a bit like giving your third grader the keys to your car. People are going to get hurt, and badly.

Now, it's true that choosing to do the right thing simply out of fear (of unpleasant consequences, of punishment, of damnation) is the *lowest* level of moral development, but some souls, including a good percentage of hormonal adolescents, need to start there. I'm going to assume that those reading this book are also filling in the other 95 percent of the story for their sons: the purpose, meaning, and beauty of human sexuality, which is infinitely attractive to a seeking human soul. But in the fallen world, we need to hit that other five percent, too, as a healthy fear can be a good motivator, helping a young man in a weak moment or dark season of life.

I want to be very clear that when my husband and I apply the "fear tactic," it is accomplished very calmly, with no hysteria or drama on our part. It is quite matter-of-fact, simple, and to the point. Let me give you some examples of this approach.

When speaking to my sons about the dangers of porn, aside from talking about its inherent sins against women and human dignity (we don't objectify, commodify, or use people), I tell them that porn is as addictive as drugs and that once a soul is drawn in and hooked, the devil has his foothold. I explain that pornography changes a man's very brain chemistry and that extricating oneself from that addiction is a brutal process, with some people not able to get out for years or decades, if ever.

I tell them how, in the "olden days," porn used to be simple photographs, two-dimensional nude women on a page, and it was not so easy for boys and teens to get ahold of. Today, porn is live, interactive, graphic, ever more perverse, depraved, and violent. It's an infinite source of virtual reality filth and exploitation, readily available at any and all moments to anyone with Internet access.

I explain that if they open the door to porn, they will crave more and more of it, in ever-darker incarnations. I tell them the truth that if they take that road, they will eventually be incapable of a healthy, normal, self-donative sexual relationship with their wives one day, and that their wives, who will be real human beings, will not be able to compete with the slick, manufactured, slavish, airbrushed women on the screen. Their wives will be crushed, neglected, rejected, and their marriages will suffer and quite possibly break apart.

After this short discussion (repeated when necessary), porn is reinforced as quite *unmanly* and beneath their own human dignity. And to give them the bright side and the hope of better things awaiting them, I remind them that according to a secular study, devout, practicing Catholics have the best sex lives![18]

LEILA MILLER

Another example of how fear of consequences can motivate: I tell my sons that sleeping with a girl before marriage could result in calamities that they have never considered. Now keep in mind that my boys are profoundly pro-life, and abortion is abhorrent to them. So, they are shaken to their core when I say, "Remember, Son, if you get a girl pregnant, there is every possibility that she will abort your child, and you will have no say in that decision. You have no legal rights at all, and you may not even find out about the pregnancy until after your child has been killed. You will have to live with that knowledge for the rest of your life." At this point, as is clear from their slacked jaws and wide eyes, they are sufficiently horrified.

I follow up with another common scenario that young men rarely consider: "If your girlfriend (or one-night stand) has your baby, and if she's not someone you end up marrying, you will still have her in your life forever, whether you like it or not. She will forever be the mother of your child, a child for whom you are responsible. You will have no say in how your child is raised (even if you get joint or partial custody, which may require considerable legal action and expense), nor will you have any control over the men or series of men and influences that will come into your child's life. There is no end to the complications that could come to all parties, especially to that innocent child who deserved—and had a right to—a married mother and father."

And, although this may not be as convincing to an immature, developing teen (the brain's frontal lobes are not fully developed until age 25), I point out that by having sex with someone out of wedlock, he could destroy a girl's trust and innocence and break her heart into a thousand pieces. Would he be able to explain that to God?

On top of it all, I remind my sons that sexual sins, if committed with full knowledge of their seriousness and with full consent of the will, can lead to eternal damnation. This is not a mere scare tactic; this is a truth of our Faith. It is unfair and unwise to shield our boys from the fact that the devil wants nothing more than to destroy innocence, poison marriages, and break apart families, all in an attempt to drag souls to hell. It's ridiculously easy for an unwarned, unguarded young man to be ensnared by sins of the flesh.

Before anyone freaks out (because frankly, I'm freaking myself out a bit by seeing the ugly truth of things laid out here in one small space), please know that Dean and I don't necessarily sit down and go over all of these points systematically in formal, austere meetings. It usually looks more like this:

We see porn discussed on TV, or we discuss pop culture, or we see a fast-food commercial that is practically soft-core porn, or I see my sons on YouTube watching something innocuous (but am reminded of the garbage that is out there), and I might say, "Just remember, porn will rewire your brain and destroy your future marriage and your life, so don't even start down that road!"

I might get the mildly annoyed "I know, Mom" in response, but often these little shout-outs open up longer conversations and we'll talk for a while. We understand each other, and they really get it, because we've woven these discussions into our everyday lives previously (late-night discussions with teens are just the best, by the way!). The boys love God, they love their faith, they love their family—including the little brothers who emulate and imitate them—and they don't want to be caught up in the sickness and sin they see all around them.

None of these interactions—whether long and involved or short and off-the-cuff—is ever done tentatively or nervously. I speak with confidence and so should you. I am the parent. This is my job. Truth-telling and formation is my duty. I am sure of these truths, and I will not be deterred, nor will I back down from my responsibilities and obligations before God.

Instilling a healthy fear of consequences can be a practical tool in your parenting toolbox. "Do not be afraid" to use it!

Now, lest you think we are a severe, gloomy, fear-based, puritanical family, read on . . . .

Chapter Ten

Navigating Pop Culture

This chapter is a tricky one. Some of the best and holiest Catholics I know, some of my dearest friends whom I admire greatly, will disagree with the Miller approach to pop culture that I am about to lay out here.

So, I offer this heartfelt caveat: Take all I say in this chapter with the understanding that *this approach works for us, but it may not be right for your family*. Each topic I will discuss is for your own family discernment. If you vehemently oppose our approach, I will not be offended; instead, I will affirm you in your own approach. God has entrusted your children to you, and you know them best. The Church is clear that *parents are the primary educators of their children*, and these parenting decisions are matters of your own prudential judgment.

For the Miller family, as imperfect as we are, here's how we do it.

Jesus told us that we Christians are to be "in the world, not of it," and we take that to heart. "The world," of course, includes a whole lot of popular culture, some of it edifying and uplifting, but much of it base and degrading. Dean and I don't shut off our kids from pop culture, but we give them the tools to discern. We make sure they know that our Catholic principles and the moral universe are not shaped or defined by any specific era, society, fad, or fashion. The virtues are the same in any culture, because they transcend every culture. It is in teaching and forming our children in virtue that we inoculate them from the corrosive effects of the particular sphere they inhabit.

Our children know well that they are allowed to live "in" the world, just as long as they realize that they do not belong to it and that their values and opinions must not be formed by it. If I were to identify one rule that we have for our children in regard to pop culture, it would be this: "If your character starts to change, that's the end of [x, y, or z] for you!"

Let's break it down by subject.

Movies/Television

I'm not going to lie; we watch a lot of television, and my husband and sons go to see a lot of movies. I know, it's probably not ideal, but that is where we are at the moment. Who am I kidding . . . that's where we've been for decades!

But even with a steady stream of popular shows and films around us, our boys have remained strong Catholics. So, how do we navigate TV and movies?

With regard to sex, this is our general rule: no overt sexuality exposure during the latency period. Shielding little ones is good and proper. When folks say that parents should not shelter their small children from the "real world," I say, "Of course we should. That's pretty much our job—to shelter them and protect their innocence."

We rarely watch the network channels anymore (thank you, Netflix), so we don't see many of the offensive commercials that could make adults blush. The little ones watch cartoons and kids' shows—until and unless those kids' shows start to showcase and promote LGBTQ+ agendas and normalization, at which point those shows are off limits in our home.

As far as movies, we don't follow a strict "no PG-13 movies until the child is 13; no R-rated movies until 17" rule. I fully respect and support those parents who do, but we take the movies on a case-by-case basis. Violence is not usually an issue in our decisions, as the context of most movie battles (good vs. evil) is okay with us. So far, we have not seen our boys become desensitized to violence, and, except for the very occasional (and normal) brotherly brawl, they have never physically fought with others.

This is not to say that we allow the all the littles to see the violent stuff as a rule; as I wrote this chapter, my husband took our 16- and 11-year-old boys to a PG-13 action movie and left the nine- and six-year-olds behind. We watched a cooking show at home while they were gone.

Just as each television show and movie is different, each

child is different. As each show is evaluated, we discern for each child as well. For example, our family tradition is for the older members of the family to watch *The Passion of the Christ* on the night of Good Friday. As you know, this R-rated movie contains graphic violence that even my own mother cannot bear to watch. One of the little boys asked us for years if he could watch with us. When he was nine years old and younger, we said no, no, no. By age 10, we let him watch all but the scourging scene (although he became tired and didn't finish the movie). Finally, at age 11, he was allowed to watch it all. He suffered no ill effects and emerged with a deeper love and appreciation for Our Lord.

With the older teens, we generally trust their judgment when they go to movies with their friends, as they have proven themselves trustworthy in this area. They usually watch whatever *Star Wars*, true war story, action, disaster, or superhero movie is out. The adults and older teens in our family do enjoy contemporary comedies and "chick flick" movies on occasion (though we skip scenes when necessary), and I will admit to a summer of binge-watching all the old *Seinfeld* seasons with my then 17-year-old son (minus a few sexually explicit episodes that I nixed). We like to bond this way in the summer evenings—our latest binge being the *Survivor* seasons, by the way. This goes back to Chapter Three and the idea that it's okay to be your child's parent *and* his friend. I love kicking back, watching, and discussing my favorite shows and movies with my friends, including my sons.

Books

When our kids are little, we try to stick with the children's classics, history and historical fiction, Catholic stories, secular biographies, saints' biographies, and other nonfiction, or innocuous entertainment including the popular series out there (*Magic Tree House, Percy Jackson*, and more). We exclude children's books that preach political correctness, identity politics, gender politics, feminist ideology, and the like. Though I read them growing up, Judy Blume books are a no-go for my kids. The *Narnia* series, *Lord of the Rings*, and other fantasy adventure books are huge favorites in the Miller house.

For the teens, we don't monitor their books that closely, and we trust their judgment until their character changes or until they give us a reason not to trust—something that hasn't happened yet. Yes, they like popular books, but they are also thoroughly immersed in the classics at their junior high and high schools, trained to recognize the true, good, and beautiful in myriad timeless works. This Great Books education not only keeps them from seeking out literary junk, but it also elevates their personal sense of virtue, character, and honor.

Music

Our younger boys don't have access to their own private devices, so they are mostly stuck listening to whatever we have on at home or in the car. By now you've guessed that we don't keep super close tabs on what the older kids listen to, but we are happy that they dislike the most vulgar offerings out there. Dean and I tend to listen to country, the Eagles, most '80s music, and popular musicals, and the kids seem to share our tastes. We, parents and children, have enjoyed singing our lungs out to the likes of REO Speedwagon, Journey, and Billy Joel while on long trips or even at a concert attended together.

While we clearly don't limit the kids to "church music" or classical offerings, we also make it very clear how today's coarse, explicit, and degrading popular songs can corrupt a soul (or a generation), and that they must avoid it. Again, I am not sure how this all works, and it might not work for your family, but here they seem to get it, so I'm sticking with it.

Computers/Internet/Phones

We have no brilliant plan here. As far as computers, no child has his own computer until he leaves for college. There is one computer in the house for everyone's use, and it's in the living room, which is centralized and a heavy traffic area. Probably due to laziness (I'm keeping it real with you), we have yet to install anti-porn filters on the computers, so I cannot weigh in on their effectiveness.

Our children earn phones on an individual basis, but none of them have had phones before junior high, and most not until high school. The first three kids had flip-phones only, and got smartphones either during college or after their engagement/

marriage. Only two of our children have had smartphones in high school, and even then, not until the upper grades. The latest son to get a smartphone got it when he could pay for it, which came the summer before his senior year.

All the minors living in our home know that any correspondence, whether by computer, email, text, or whatever, is subject to parental reading and review at any time. We are not zealously checking, but they are all aware that there is no "privacy" in our home when a child's safety (body or soul) is involved. Everything is open to inspection.

Video Games

Personally, I despise the male culture of video games. I am a hypocrite in some ways, however, as I love to play my own pet games on my phone. But there is something about seeing boys, teens, and young men playing on that stupid machine for hours and hours that makes me want to explode into irrational fits of anger (and I may or may not have done so once or twice . . . ish . . .). Of course it's not the boys' fault; my husband and I are the parents after all, and aside from imposing some long hiatuses, we have not (yet!) permanently pulled the plug.

My advice is standard: Limit your sons' playing time, or better yet, never get a video gaming system to begin with. Read Richard Louv's *Last Child in the Woods* for some motivation and courage if you need it.

There is something I want to mention that you might not

have heard before, though. Video games can be a way to let off steam and work off tension, a good avenue of distraction for those boys who are otherwise hardworking. Specifically for chaste young men, it's better that they have a video game with which to unwind and de-stress, as opposed to Internet porn. Before his marriage, my oldest son lived alone in a small apartment in a tiny town two thousand miles from his family. As a medical student, he would study long hours, eat in solitude, and often find himself quite lonely. He has told me that his video gaming (usually played live with his younger brothers across the country) was an excellent way to keep the temptation for sexual impurity and porn usage at bay.

Also, video games that stress heroism and conquering evil are not an inherently bad way to allow a boy or young man to express his warrior spirit in a culture that tells him he should not be a fierce protector nor fight the battles for good.

These are points worth considering as we make our family decisions and as we (bottom line) protect against the scourge of gaming addiction.

Schools

When it comes to schools, we have done it all: private secular schooling, private Catholic schooling, homeschooling, public charter schooling, regular public schooling, community college, state universities, etc.

In the early years of our decision-making, I remember being so relieved that "This is it!" and that there would never be a change in our schooling plan. Then God laughed and changed the plan—again and again and again. We have gotten to the point where we never say never about what type of school our children will attend. Each child is different, each school is different, and no school is perfect. We are grateful to have so many options today, and this is particularly true in Arizona, where choice in education is a tremendous blessing. Over a quarter-century into parenting now and with many years to go (our youngest is a first grader), we have learned to take things year by year, and sometimes semester by semester.

As far as the specifics of making school decisions, Dean and I are not closed to the feelings and input of our children, but we, and not the child, have the final say. I suppose I could write a book on the different schools and approaches we've taken over the years, but suffice to say that as long as your child is being catechized well, lives his faith, and is of good character, you are on the right track. If not, make a change.

Ideally, I would love to see every child receive a Great Books, classical, Catholic education, but that is not always possible. I've learned that, as long as a child is strong, secure, and joyful in his Catholic Faith, he can become the light of Christ to others, leavening whatever schooling environment he inhabits. I've seen it happen firsthand, and not just with my own kids.

So, moms, don't beat yourself up if you cannot provide the "perfect" school environment for your children at all times. Do your best, watch your children's character, and make adjustments when necessary. Take every child and every school year as they come, and stay in Christ's peace.

Dating

My children did not do a lot of dating in high school, and, in fact, only one child (our oldest daughter) had a steady boyfriend for a couple of years of chaste dating. The young man was a family friend and a practicing Catholic, and parents on both sides approved. My boys never really dated at all, aside from asking young women to homecoming or prom—often at my insistence, as I strongly believe that no gentleman should leave any young lady without a date to the big dance!

My feelings on teen dating are not set in stone, and we don't forbid it, but for some reason it's just never really been an issue. My three oldest children married young by today's standards, so when they did date, they dated with the purpose of finding a Catholic spouse and starting a family. We did not force or browbeat them into young marriages, and, although we *very strongly* encouraged them to date only faithful Catholics, there was no guillotine hanging over their heads. They chose that, and it's what they desired (thanks be to God) after being raised in the way that we've discussed in this book so far.

Now, I do have a million and one opinions on the adult Catholic dating/marriage scene in general, but that's a whole other book!

Friends

One of the best things we ever did after my reversion and Dean's conversion was to find a community of like-minded, serious Catholic families. This provided our family—both parents and children—with a set of solid Catholic friends. For us, that community came by way of a tiny independent parent-run Catholic school that, although not a diocesan school, had the blessing of our bishop. The deep, faith-based friendships that we and our children made there have lasted to this day.

Back in those early days, after we transitioned from living a largely secular life to a life of faith, it was a joy for us to see our children experiencing the Catholic culture as their norm. Families with five, seven, and even 10 kids were just typical families to them. We worshipped God together at Mass, the saints were heavenly friends and role models, and a kid could go play at another kid's house without fear of conflicting values. I am forever grateful for our many years at not one, but two such Catholic schools, which felt like extended family.

Now that I'm an older and more seasoned mother, and now that my current littles have plenty of faithful older siblings as role models, a change in circumstance does not trouble my spirit. As I type this, not a single one of our children is attending Catholic school (though our youngest will be headed to one next year), and most of their classmates are not Catholic. As our family has grown big enough to be a society unto itself, and as we keep close to families from our old schools and current parishes, the younger children have enough support to sustain their Catholic beliefs, even as they enjoy their new friends. There are good kids everywhere, and character attracts character. So, know your child, know his friends, and make adjustments accordingly.

As you can see, our approach to navigating pop culture is not completely ordered, and we don't have a seamless plan. Let's face it: We are winging much of it as we go along! No doubt many of you have an even better plan for your family, one that has fewer gaps than ours. The most important thing is to pray often, stick to some basic principles that work ("when a child's character starts to change, we make a change"), and be at peace. God honors our efforts more than we realize.

When my kids become adults and move out of the house (as my fifth child is about to do), I "let them go" as best I can from an emotional and control standpoint, trusting that the foundation we gave them is strong. All praise to God, the foundation has held steady for those who have already left the nest, and I pray every day that it will continue that way for the rest of the children coming up the line.

There is one kind of damage that popular culture (and political correctness) can cause our sons, however, which must be squarely faced and rejected. We will tackle that next . . . .

Chapter Eleven

Training Men Out of Manhood

Many of the dangers our sons face are easy enough to spot. The red flags of early sexualization, the hookup culture, pornography, and moral relativism make themselves clear enough.

But there is something more subtle that traps our boys. It's a steady drumbeat of dismissal, disdain, condescension, and disposability of men's unique gifts, contributions, and innate masculine nature. I call this "training men out of manhood," and it's insidious.

As an example, a feminist activist who blogs at *Plain Jane Activism* proudly identified herself as a mother who "regularly annoys her six-year-old son by staging peace talks with his action figures, and by grounding him whenever he attempts to rescue a princess."[19] My heart broke when I read this! This primal, vital, God-given instinct of a boy to be protector, provider, and hero is disparaged and made grounds for punishment by the first woman in his life.

While the attempt at some kind of social consciousness here may be well-meaning, this mother's approach is tragically misguided. Every boy and man wants to charge into battle as the knight in shining armor ready to defeat the evil villain for a noble and righteous cause. Good vs. evil is the thrilling, ultimate battle, not only temporally but also in the spiritual realm. The masculine heart is made for such things, and a small boy starts his training young.

And, oh, the desire to rescue the damsel in distress should be cultivated! In this culture where so many women and children look in vain for good and protective men, why would we discourage our boys' intuitive desire to willingly sacrifice themselves for others, especially women and children who are in danger? If we dampen (or, worse yet, punish) this instinct in men and boys, we risk killing the part of them that gives them purpose and mission. In fact, we deaden the very instinct that puts the "gentle" in "gentleman." Who wants a man unwilling to save the fair maiden but instead is quick to save his own hide? What is so terrible about "women and children first"? If chivalry is dead, it's largely because too many feminists, and even misguided Christians, willfully extinguished the protective instincts in their sons.

Our boys are floundering from too many cultural blows to their masculine identity. They need to be shown the path to manhood by other men, and when fathers are missing in their lives, as is so often the case today, we find many lost boys. Women, we can't take the place of men, but our boys do need us to understand and encourage the nature of a man.

As one of my favorite Catholic writers, Professor Anthony Esolen, says in one of his many brilliant essays on boyhood and manhood:

> A woman who would lead boys must somehow see in them the fathers-to-be, the leaders of other men; and this involves her in some difficulty. She wants to raise sons to be men who protect women, and who would not use their considerable advantage in strength and in tolerance for aggression and danger to put women at risk. But she cannot inspire boys with the noble calling of protector and provider while assuring them that they are no different from their sisters . . . .[20]

God Himself made male and female different. I had the privilege of sitting on the original working panel for Bishop Olmsted's *Into the Breach*. One of the presenters was Dr. Deborah Savage, a professor at Saint Paul Seminary in Minnesota, who made a point that pretty much blew my mind and has stayed with me ever since: In the Book of Genesis, "man's first contact with reality is of a horizon that otherwise contains only lower creatures, what we might call 'things.' . . . Woman comes into existence after man, [and] her first contact with reality is of a horizon that, from the beginning, includes man, that is, it includes persons. . . . Other creatures and things around her appear only on the periphery of her gaze."[21]

This realization spurred and confirmed my understanding that we women are naturally relational and more oriented toward people, while men are more naturally oriented toward things and tasks. As Dr. Savage explains, men have a gifted capacity for understanding how to use the goods of creation to protect and provide for family and society. Neither disposition is better or worse, as each speaks to the respective genius of female and male. If we take away the particular "task" of man and his sense of mission—if he has no land to subdue, castles to build, or battles to win—we take away part of who he is, and he shrivels to something less than what a man was created to be. Women, and especially mothers: We must not diminish our boys' God-given sense of mission and identity!

I have no problem with my boys doing sword play or simulating duels or using fake guns. Cops and robbers, slaying dragons, or dreams of joining the military to "fight the bad guys" might be objectionable for some, but I don't discourage it.

One of the best conversations I have ever heard (and, I promise, the only one on which I've ever seriously eavesdropped) was between my two oldest sons as they talked in their room late one night before bed. My older son was home from college, and the two young men were discussing self-sacrifice, dying heroically, and even the possibility of martyrdom. When my 17-year-old kept insisting that there is no more honorable or even glorious way for a man to die than to lay down his life for another (throwing himself in front of a bullet for a stranger, came as one example), my maternal heart leapt with joy. Far from being anxious or worried about his desire, I felt so much peace interiorly, and gratitude to God for making great and noble the heart of my son.

I have never met a married woman who does not want her husband to take care of her and protect her. And I don't mean that she wants no voice, that she wants to be a helpless little girl who can't do anything for herself, or that she wants to be dominated or controlled. The women I know are very strong, capable, and intelligent—nobody's fools. But when many of these same strong women hit rough patches in their marriages, they complain that their husbands are not "being the man." In fact, the exact words of many of these women are as follows: "I am tired of being the man. I need him to step up. I need to be taken care of sometimes. I want to feel like and be treated like a woman."

Think about that. None of these women are products of strict gender role-modeling from a 1950s detergent commercial. They are women raised in the '70s, '80s, and '90s, when "women's liberation" was already in full swing.

A while back, I wrote a piece in which I identified three types of men who support abortion. The first two—"the ignorant apathetic" and "the lech (or cad, or reprobate, etc.)"—are interesting to ponder, but it's the third category that is the most tragic in my mind: "the man trained out of manhood."

To illustrate this man, I took former President Barack Obama as an example. I don't mean to pick on him, but to me he is representative of so many other men raised and formed under similar circumstances. He is a man so lacking in the male protective instinct that he is fiercely committed to abortion at any stage and situation, *even to the point of voting to let a child die who survives abortion.*[22] How could this be? It makes sense if we consider his upbringing. As I said in the article:

> Obama was raised by a radical-leftist-secular-feminist-socialist mother. His father wanted nothing to do with little Barack, essentially abandoning him and becoming simply a myth and a longing in young Barack's life and dreams. It's actually incredibly tragic to ponder, truly heartbreaking.
>
> So, this fatherless boy was not raised to know what it means to be a strong man who stays, protects, provides. He had no idea, and in fact the opposite was modeled to him by his absent, negligent father. Meantime, he had his strong, outspoken, and deeply committed feminist mother who taught him what a "man" should be, according to her radical template. Obama himself has described his mother, Stanley Ann Dunham, as "the dominant figure in my formative years . . . . The values she taught me continue to be my touchstone when it comes to how I go about the world of politics."[23] He called her "a lonely witness for secular humanism."[24]
>
> Not surprisingly, he grew up and married another strong radical feminist, Michelle Robinson. Both these

women were the dominant forces in his life, and they no doubt pounded it home to him that women have an absolute right to abortion. I'd be surprised if Barack Obama has ever had a true friendship with a strong pro-life woman, or even meaningful interaction with one. But the message he received time and again from all the women in his life—the woman who raised and formed him, the woman who married him, and even the radical women he hung out with at Columbia and later in politics—goes like this: "You *men* have no right to tell us women what to do with our bodies. We have a right to abortion on demand and without apology. You are either with us on this most basic of freedoms, or you are a misogynist brute oppressor."

What is a fatherless, lonely, ungrounded boy/man to do? I can hardly blame men like this, because, at least for a time, they simply don't know any better. They defer to the women they love regarding "women's issues" and "women's bodies" and "justice for women" because they really believe it's not their place to speak. These men really believe that this is how one "supports" women (*Little Catholic Bubble*, January 27, 2016).

Much like the six-year-old son of the blogger I mentioned at the top of this chapter, feeling shame about being a male is what will drive our boys and men to snuff out or reject their natural and rightly-ordered instincts to be protectors, providers, leaders, and heroes. These men, in increasing numbers, have perhaps never seen a truly honorable man up close and active in their lives. Perhaps they have never known a male role model who keeps his commitments, protects and defends women and children, and is willing to lay down his own life for them before he'd consider harming them, body or soul.

The man trained out of manhood champions abortion, "gay marriage," "gender fluidity," no-fault divorce, and the radical feminism of today because he believes that's what he's supposed to do if he cares about women and humanity. He is left with an impoverished masculinity, and the whole world suffers for it.

Ladies, we have an important role to play: We must rejoice and affirm our boys when they want to engage in fake sword play with their brothers and friends. We must encourage the "hero" posturing and good guy vs. bad guy scenarios they dream up, even if the good guy wins by pretending to punch the bad guy in the nose, or by taking him out via dueling pistols in the Wild West. (One of my favorite home videos is an elaborate dueling scene between two of my then little boys, filmed by their older brother, unbeknownst to me at the time. We all laugh about it and enjoy it to this day.)

When we allude to "boys will be boys" in my house, it doesn't mean anything like what today's feminists assume, i.e., license for boys to be oppressors, rapists, or wife beaters. Nor does it mean what some fellow Christians say, that "hey, of course boys will be masturbating, looking at porn, and having premarital sex, no big deal." In our house, it means that boys will naturally want to play the hero warrior, fight to protect the innocent, and defeat the bad guy. We could say more accurately that that's how boys will be men.

The precipitous decline in marriage and family life among our young men is a societal crisis, largely due to a lack of manly virtue. The aspiration for marriage, family, and fatherhood is strong in a virtuous young man and should be encouraged. As Pope Francis told the throngs of young people in Rio at World Youth Day on July 28, 2013:

> Today, there are those who say that marriage is out of fashion; in a culture of relativism and the ephemeral, many preach the importance of "enjoying" the moment. They say that it is not worth making a lifelong commitment, making a definitive decision, "forever," because we do not know what tomorrow will bring.
>
> I ask you, instead, to be **revolutionaries**, to swim against the tide; yes, I am asking you to **rebel against this culture** that sees everything as temporary and that ultimately believes that you are incapable of responsibility, that you are incapable of true love. I have confidence in you and I pray for you. Have the courage "to swim against the tide"; have the courage to be happy (emphases mine).

The Holy Father wants our children to be rebels for marriage! Parents, encourage this "rebellious" desire if you see it in your sons!

Even if a man never actually marries and has children of his own, the desire itself is healthy and right. Again from Pope Francis, in his homily of June 26, 2013:

When a man does not have this desire, something is missing in this man. Something is wrong. All of us, to exist, to become complete, in order to be mature, we need to feel the joy of fatherhood: even those of us who are celibate. Fatherhood is giving life to others, giving life, giving life . . . (*Morning Meditation*).

And from Bishop Olmsted's *Into the Breach*:

Like masculinity itself, perhaps fatherhood has never been a widely pondered topic among the philosophers because it has always been presumed, its meaning fairly obvious. This is no longer true. In his book, *Crossing the Threshold of Hope*, Saint John Paul II writes of the attack on fatherhood in modern society: "This is truly the key for interpreting reality [...] **original sin, then, attempts to abolish fatherhood.**" The great pontiff of the family points to our first parents' original act of disobedience, which cost them and us our original innocence and freedom from bodily death, and in original sin, we find a primordial rebellion against God's fatherhood, a desire to remove fatherhood itself. This is our enemy's underlying plan: to remove our reliance on God, the benevolent Father. To do this, **Satan's primary strategy is to damage and**

abolish human fatherhood, in the man and relationship where each of us first glimpses what God's fatherhood might be like.

Also:

There are those in our culture today, however, who do not want us to see fatherlessness as unnatural or lamentable. **Do not be fooled by those voices wishing to erase all distinctions between mothers and fathers, ignoring the complementarity that is inherent in creation itself"** (all emphases mine).

We have a task ahead as we raise our sons to understand their own mission and identity *as men*. We must never concede even one inch to those who would have us train our men out of their very manhood.

Is this all just a pipe dream, though? Are there really any young men out there anymore who are strong and courageous enough to swim against the tide and embrace chastity and true masculinity? Oh, yes! Prepare to have your hope renewed as I introduce you to a few good men . . . .

Chapter Twelve

Advice From Chaste Young Men

I asked several chaste young men, including my three oldest sons, for their answers to five questions:

1. What is the biggest challenge you face in this culture with regard to chastity?
2. Why do you remain chaste when others don't?
3. What do you say to those who would insist that you are lying about being chaste?
4. What advice do you have for (worried) parents who are trying to raise chaste boys?
5. What is your advice for boys/men trying to navigate this unchaste culture?

I wanted my sons to be totally honest and unguarded, and boy, were they—especially my oldest son. He pulled no punches, and I'm grateful for his honesty. His tone is firm and might seem too blunt for some of us mommies, but he is speaking the language that young men can hear (I even asked a few young men to read it first—they had no problem with it, even those who have struggled with these sins). If you consider boot camp in the military, there is a reason why the drill sergeants speak to the (mostly male) recruits that way. They hear tough talk from a man who's trying to whip them into shape, and they respond.

My oldest son is speaking as one who has "battled the beast up close," and he made it clear to me that he is directing these words to practicing Catholics, *not* to those young men who know nothing about the Faith and the moral law.

Here is what he wrote as 22-year-old (prior to his marriage):

1. What is the biggest challenge you face in this culture with regard to chastity?

The biggest challenge is the constant temptation. The Internet has unlimited amounts of pornography and erotica that is easily accessible. I live alone; there is no one to hold me accountable. I have to hold myself accountable. Despite actively avoiding this material on the Internet, I will still sometimes find it unwittingly. This is the true challenge: to click that red X at the top of the screen before I lose my rationality. The other aspect of this is that in every modern medium, premarital sex and masturbation are treated as common everyday things that everyone is and should be doing. I once went to a urologist, and he told me point blank that I should be masturbating— that it was normal! When I was younger, this used to make me feel very weird and different from my friends. It made me feel like an outcast. However, I no longer feel that way—I am not so easily swayed by peer pressure and have since realized that these people are slaves to their desires often in the same way animals are.

2. Why do you remain chaste when others don't?

Multiple reasons:

a. I have a true understanding of the purpose of sexual faculties. That it is to be both unitive and procreative, and that any misuse of this is a grave sin. Sex is not just about pleasure for pleasure's sake. It is giving the whole of yourself to another in sacrificial love. Any distortion of this act is inherently selfish and immoral.

b. I view masturbation as one of the most pathetic and harmful things a person can do to himself, and as such I avoid it. To me it is childish and just plain gross. Why would I want to have sex with my hand? We are not made for it; we are made for something much more beautiful. It follows that since I despise masturbation so, I would remain chaste.

c. I have a fear of hell and of offending God. It is such a profound fear that I would never even consider masturbating or having premarital relations.

3. What do you say to those who would insist that you are lying about being chaste?

I probably wouldn't say anything. They can think what they want; it does not affect what is true. However, for the purpose of the question, I guess I would ask them: Why would

I even lie about such a thing? If masturbation and sex are so normal and commonplace, why would I want to appear the outsider? Why, if 97 percent of men are [masturbating] daily, would I put myself in the three percent that don't? Why would I make myself look like a freak?

4. What advice do you have for (worried) parents who are trying to raise chaste boys?

From the start, have an open-door policy with your boys. No question should ever be off limits. Do not shame them for wondering, and do not chastise them for being curious about the female form. When I was younger, about 12, I was on Amazon, and a photography book that had a naked woman on the cover caught my eye. I clicked on it and stared at the pictures until my mother caught me. I was ashamed, obviously, but she thought it more funny than anything. The point is: She did not shame me or punish me; she explained that I should not view such things and, more importantly, WHY I should not view them. Always give a reason, and if you don't know why, find out! You will earn their respect and trust, and they will always come to you first with questions.

Do not be afraid to teach basic female anatomy to your sons at around the time you have "the talk" with them. If you do not teach them about this stuff, they will inevitably take to the Internet to find out for themselves and may be exposed to some very nasty stuff in the process. Teach them that the naked human body is not something to be feared or disrespected.

5. What is your advice for other boys/men trying to navigate this unchaste culture?

Stop touching it. Seriously, control yourselves. The act of masturbation requires many steps, all of which, at any point, you can stop. In the same way, the act of premarital sex requires conscious choices. You don't "accidentally" have sex. You are called to be strong men, not juvenile children hiding in their closets. If your computer leads you to sin, smash it. Rise up; you are not a slave to your passions. You are a man with free will. You have the power to choose. And remember that you have no legitimate excuse for your actions. We will always try to justify our sins, since we are human after all. But your justifications are as pathetic and harmful as the act you are about to inflict upon yourself. Be a strong, God-fearing, selfless man.

Next, my 18-year-old son gave his responses:

1. The biggest challenge I face in the culture is probably that everyone just accepts unchastity to be normal. Everywhere on TV or at school, people present these sins as something that everyone does or something everyone should do. I've never been unchaste or sinned sexually, so it's not that hard for me to maintain that. It's not hard to continue *not* doing something. The law of inertia applies here: An object at rest tends to stay at rest. So, don't start masturbating in the first place and you'll have a much easier time. It's annoying that the culture today is so tolerant of such things and assumes that if everyone is doing it then it must be okay.

2. I remain chaste because I know it's a sin and understand why it's a sin. A lot of people probably have been told that it's wrong, but not *why* it's wrong. If it's not harming anyone, how could it be wrong? Telling someone it's wrong is not enough. It is important to understand why, in order to know that you shouldn't do it. That holds true for all sins.

3. If people think I'm lying about my chastity, it makes me disappointed that people think I can't have self-control. Other than that, I'm not bothered by it because God knows that I'm chaste and that's all that matters anyway. People are allowed to be wrong.

4. For parents, I would say trust your kids. Give them the benefit of the doubt. If you have explained to them why these acts are sinful, it should be enough to keep them chaste. After you teach them why it is a sin, it's really out of your hands whether or not they keep their morals. It's between them and God.

5. For other boys and men, stay strong in the face of society. Prove everyone else wrong. It will pay off in the end. Waiting until marriage to experience sexual pleasure is probably the best way to experience it. Don't ruin that. It's not how God made us.

And from my 15-year-old son (funny how the words are fewer the younger they get):

1. My biggest challenge is when I see an attractive person, I try not to think of lustful things. It's easy to think of lustful things, so I challenge myself not to.

2. I first find other things or hobbies to keep my mind

occupied. Also, I would never want to [have to] say those sins to a priest in confession, so it helps keep me in check.

3. I would tell them that I'm not lying, but they can think whatever they want to think.

4. There is nothing you can do to stop your kids. But teach them right from wrong and hopefully they will make the right decision.

5. Try to find other things to occupy your mind. It is very easy to sin, so find something else to replace it.

I was also able to ask several other young men from around the country the same questions. Their answers are incredibly hopeful and, I believe, helpful.

In response to the first question, **"What is the biggest challenge you face in this culture with regard to chastity?"**

From a 22-year-old engaged man:

When I was in college, I remember my roommates and I throwing a party at our house for Super Bowl XLIX. Keep in mind that the Super Bowl is the biggest television event in the United States every year, with most of the viewers being a male audience. During the halftime show, Katy Perry initially came out dressed in clothes that covered her body more than usual. This prompted one of my roommates to exclaim something along the lines of, "She's wearing too much clothing! I can't see any of her!"

Those two sentences really summed up our culture in a nutshell. Much to my roommate's delight, and to my dismay, Katy Perry didn't stay like that and she gradually took off much of her clothing as the show went on. This is what we are up against. We have a culture that expects women to act like sex objects while men can continue to indulge themselves in their lustful fantasies. What my roommate said was very symbolic of our age: down with chastity and up with lust.

From a 16-year-old star high school athlete:
The biggest challenge for me is the influence from my friends/students/teammates.

From a 22-year-old who is "loving chastity":
Advertisements. Most advertisements are porn. They don't sell a product, they sell sex (or sex is the product). Throw in movies and TV shows. All of these things are more often than not pornified. These things are all the propaganda of an unchaste culture.

From a 24-year-old engaged man:
Because I was open about believing—as the Church does—in abstinence before marriage, I was ridiculed by males and patronized by females. The feeling, thus promoted by society, that one is not a real man unless he is having a lot of sex and is very good at it, can be a huge challenge for a young man trying to maintain his virtue.

From a 23-year-old Catholic seminarian:

Temptations toward unchastity are literally everywhere! The most challenging thing is that, while there are certainly a lot of overt sexual themes on TV and in movies and advertising, the temptations and the things that lead to unchastity are usually much more covert. The constant promotion of individuality, of moral relativism, and the necessary indulgence of every desire (carnal or otherwise) create a culture in which anything goes and everything is acceptable.

From an 18-year-old Catholic seminarian:

By far the biggest obstacle to young men striving to be chaste is the omnipresence of suggestive material in everyday life. Many chastity speakers and writers emphasize the destructive nature of things such as TV commercials and magazine covers, but the impact of images on the minds of boys simply cannot be conveyed in a few words. For me in our current culture, normal activities like watching a football game or buying groceries become mentally excruciating and spiritually dangerous.

From a 15-year-old high school student:

Being a student at a public high school, many of my peers often ask if I want to view nudes of any of the various women on campus. The hardest thing to do is tell them no, not only because I am often tempted to view them, but also because of peer pressure, which can seem worse than the temptation of looking at the photos.

From a 22-year-old man:

For me, I have found the biggest challenge lies in how our culture tells women to behave. I have, on more than one occasion, had to call things off with a girlfriend because she felt that sex needed to be part of our relationship. The "everyone else is doing it" mentality has certainly been ingrained into men and women in our society, and that can be challenging for men such as me. I won't lie and say that calling things off was easy; in fact, I was engaged to one of these women, but a strong foundation and constant support from my family helped.

From a 24-year-old man:

The most difficult part is the influence of peers and culture being thrown in your face. The fact that you have to face it when you do anything. Even in your own home on the TV and computer. You'd have to become a hermit to avoid it, and even that is difficult. To function in society you must be exposed to sexually explicit material. Because we have become accustomed to little things like mild jokes and whatnot, we don't even know we are being weakened.

In response to the fourth question: **"What advice do you have for (worried) parents who are trying to raise chaste boys?"**

From a 22-year-old engaged man:

When boys are educated in chastity, it needs to be done in a way of understanding about their bodies, and it should be open enough for them to ask questions. If the education is too harsh, they may become ashamed of their bodies, even if there was nothing to be ashamed about in the first place. If the education is too lax—or worse, if there is no education—then the boys will learn from the culture. It is also important that it is not a onetime "talk" and nothing else. The education needs to be continuous, since boys progress through more body changes as they grow older. The communication line must be kept open so that they are comfortable to ask questions whenever they have them.

From a 16-year-old star high school athlete:

Raise your kids in a faith-filled environment. And allow your kids to open up to the Faith. Send them to youth conferences like Steubenville. This transformed my faith from something you have to do into something you want to do.

From a 22-year-old who is "loving chastity":

Do not worry. Do not be afraid. Talk to your boys about sex and love, and do not shy away from it. I know many parents who decided not to talk to their children about sex until they are such-and-such an age, and even then it's a onetime, vague conversation about "the birds and the bees." When this happens, your children will learn more about sex from their friends at school and teachers in health classes than from you.

Sex is beautiful; love is amazing! I know you think sex is amazing and beautiful! Why do you shy away from telling your kids about it? Do not make the "sex talk" a onetime thing. Make it a continual conversation, starting when they are young. Most importantly, though, love your spouse. Wives, kiss your husbands, husbands kiss your wives in front of your kids. Let them see the affection you show each other. Show them how devoted you are to each other. Show them how you chastely live in marriage. This is an infinitely better lesson than using words.

From a 23-year-old Catholic seminarian:

Don't try to hide the culture from them or them from the culture; when they inevitably go out into the world they won't be ready for it, first of all, and second, their reaction will be like a broken spring: The tightness that once protected them will turn into the force of their demise.

Set clear rules about technology use, acceptable behavior with women, but don't criminalize their sexuality. So: culture of chastity, openness with your kids about their struggles, and nonjudgmentalism.

From an 18-year-old Catholic seminarian:

If you as parents see or sense worldliness or an unchaste spirit in a peer or companion, ensure that your child parts ways with the young person. Do not be afraid of appearing harsh or unreasonable. It took me 17 years to encounter chaste and godly men for friends, but such blessings they have been to me that I would go back and wait to meet them anew.

From a 22-year-old man:

My biggest word of advice would be to establish a strong sense of communication. I have always felt that I can come to my parents with any questions or problems I have had, and that has certainly helped. As I mentioned before, I had to call off an engagement with a woman I had been in a relationship with for many years, and this was because of, among other things, an issue of chastity. The communication my parents offered to me helped me through this process more than I can ever say, and I can't thank them enough for it. I think with a strong line of communication, parents can convey a strong message of chastity that will permanently be instilled in their boys.

From a young married man looking back on his single years:

I would tell parents to talk about chastity in age-appropriate ways, starting as early as the age of reason and not shrinking from the subject, especially when they become awkward teenagers.

From a 24-year-old man:

This one is very difficult. Obviously the first and most important thing is for parents to pray. I've seen many good parents have children become sex addicts and leave the Faith. On a side note, most young people I've known have left the faith for sexual reasons. They slept with someone, decided not to go to confession, and that was it. I think if parents lead a good example and don't obsessively enforce it, children naturally will follow them.

There is so much more that these good—and utterly nor-mal—young men have to say. Those of you with older boys might want to refer them to the webpage[25] where I have posted all their advice for young men, which was too long to include here. I will leave you with a couple of their gems of wisdom specifically directed to your sons:

Take the long and narrow road. Find good and en-couraging friends, men and women, to keep your per-spective clean. Do not waver in the face of adversity, because if you do, you will be less of the man that you were created to be—and to get back that which was lost is a rough and rugged road. You will not die if you do not give in; trust me.

Above all, be courageous, and be such a man that other men will look at you and say, "Christ abides in him; I wish to possess this fire also."

Despite our best efforts, however, sometimes things go wrong . . . .

Chapter Thirteen

When Things Go Wrong

After all your blood, sweat, and tears, and after countless hours in supplication to God and His mother for your children, it could be that your son will grow to adolescence and regularly commit sins against chastity. Maybe that's already happened. Before you fall into guilt, self-reproach, anger, anxiety, depression, or despair, memorize these two hard and fast rules:

Rule No. 1: Do not freak out!

Rule No. 2: Refer to Rule No. 1.

Freaking out will accomplish absolutely nothing, and you want to stay away from anything that is nonproductive.

Your job at this point is to remain steadfast in the truths of your Catholic Faith while staying available and open to communication. Continue to show affection and love to your child, no matter what he has done. God does not love us with conditions, nor does He abandon us when we sin, and so we must follow His example of unconditional love for our own sinful children,

125

who are still and always precious to us, made in the image and likeness of God. Remember, though, that loving and cherishing him *does not in any way mean accepting, condoning, enabling, or encouraging his sins.*

Most importantly, your job is to pray. A call to prayer may sound trite and useless when a beloved child seems happy with (or addicted to) his sin, but nothing could be further from the truth. It is in this situation that you, dear mother, are a modern-day Saint Monica. She prayed many long years for her wayward adult son, Augustine, whose Achilles' heel was lust. He was unable or unwilling to fight the beast of unchastity for what must have seemed like an eternity to his poor mother. He lived with and used women, fathered a child out of wedlock, and still came to be one of the Church's greatest bishops and saints, a champion of chastity, and a Doctor of the Church. He credited his mother's prayers as key to bringing him from darkness to light. She was despairing of hope for her son, until a saintly bishop advised her that "the son of so many tears could not perish."

Far too many stories of conversion fill Christian history and even our own little spheres of life to despair of any soul, much less our own precious sons caught up in their sins. The story of sin and redemption is, in fact, the story of humanity itself. To save us from our wretched sins is the very reason Jesus Christ came in the flesh and died on the Cross! Though we'd never consciously want to push it this far, our Faith teaches us that we each have until our last breath to repent and turn to God, and that the Lord will give us all the graces necessary to do so. We need only choose to cooperate with those graces.

For those of you who do not have a supportive spouse (or any spouse at all) by your side in this fight, remember that Saint Monica was alone in her fight for her son as well. Saint Augustine's father was a pagan until late in his life, when he finally accepted baptism and went to a holy death, thanks to the influence and example of his ever-faithful wife.

Without the benefit of a healthy, happy marriage serving as an example to your children and creating a unified front for your sons, the task of raising chaste young men is certainly more difficult. But we know as Christians that the task is not impossible; it simply means you'll have to double down on making the Faith seem reasonable and stable in a world gone mad.

Our Catholic Faith is the shelter in a storm, the one thing that will never change and that your son can always count on, even if his own family has been rocked with uncertainty, lack of stability, confusion, and pain. It is precisely for the lost, the wounded, and the broken that Christ came. The healthy have no need of a physician, after all.

The Church, including her teachings on chastity, is balm for the wounded soul. She is the rock-solid foundation for the boy who feels like he's been placed on shifting sand as a fatherless male or a child of divorce. The attraction to the Church is potentially even bigger in your household than in others, because it's a golden lifeline of truth and hope offered to a young man who is at greater risk of sinking in cultural quicksand.

My husband was raised in a secular Jewish household,

witnessed decades of his parents' always-unhappy marriage, and was not schooled in the virtue of chastity (quite the opposite, in fact). If we speak of ideal conditions for understanding and embracing that particular virtue, the deck was stacked against Dean a mile high.

However, a small, still voice in all of us speaks of timeless truths and the dignity of our own humanity. We were made for more than pleasure-seeking and comfort, and somewhere inside, every boy and every man knows this.

Something in Dean held him back from being the cad that he easily could have been, and by the time we discovered the fullness of Catholicism together (after six years of marriage and three children), he was ready to embrace the virtues enthusiastically. And, as evidence that we can never know the full depth, breadth, and beauty of God's plan, a full 20 years later Dean helped to lead his Jewish/agnostic/New Age divorced mother to Christ. Partly due to the example of her son and our family, Carol was baptized, confirmed, and received Jesus in the Eucharist in August 2013. And after having lived the majority of her 67 years without God, she died a holy death with the sacraments of the Church just 15 months after her conversion.[26] God is good, and He is pleased to work with our wounds and weaknesses to bring about grace-filled miracles for His glory.

There are specific and practical things that can help you as a mother without a supportive spouse. Michael Phelan, the director of the Marriage and Respect Life Office for the Diocese of Phoenix, who has dedicated his life to addressing the crisis of manhood, has this advice to share:

Remember that God has not abandoned you or your son, even if the husband/father has. Embrace the "work of trust in God" necessary and make time to become true and wise disciples of the Lord, and to heal where needed. You especially must not take shallow and harmful solace in dating other men until they have experienced significant healing. You are called to radical trust, deep discipleship, and holiness in the face of difficult odds.

Though you are a true, true hero for your stalwart presence with your children, you cannot be a father, and you should not embrace the silly cultural illusion that you can be. You must pray hard and look to ask healthy men who have time to be father figures for your children, especially your boys.

And to men reading this: It is time for a movement of healthy fathers and grandfathers at parishes to step into this breach and provide counsel, time, and a fatherly model to these abandoned and "at risk" boys. These boys and their mothers are the "widows and orphans" of our time, and God is calling us to step up (Personal interview by the author, June 2016).

It is imperative that you not despair for lack of a perfect situation (remember that discouragement is from the devil, never from Christ), but answer the call to personal holiness, wisdom, and knowledge; take every opportunity to make yourself an amateur expert on the teachings of human sexuality, on the vision of the Church, and on the design of God's creation. Be sure to enlist others around you for support.

And a word for those wayward or missing fathers, if any are reading this, from Bishop Olmsted's *Into the Breach*:

> Catholic men also contribute far too regularly to this same scandal that devastates the heart of a child and makes too many women in our culture live as if they were widows! The ache of the fatherless child's heart cries out to Heaven: "He will not ignore the supplication of the fatherless, nor the widow when she pours out her story . . . and the Lord will not delay, neither will He be patient with them, till He crushes the loins of the unmerciful and repays vengeance on the nations" (Sirach 35:14, 18). Why do the widows and the fatherless cry out? They have lost their protectors and providers! There is an unnatural void of the one called upon by God "to ensure the harmonious and united development of all the members of the family." It is because of this loss, this void caused by men's absence that we have always naturally, traditionally, lamented fatherlessness.
>
> . . . Men, your presence and mission in the family is irreplaceable! Step up and lovingly, patiently take up your God-given role as protector, provider, and spiritual leader of your home. A father's role as spiritual head of the family must never be understood or undertaken as domination over others, but only as a loving leadership

and a gentle guidance for those in your care. Your fatherhood . . . in its hidden, humble way, reflects imperfectly but surely the fatherhood of God, the Father to those whom the Lord has given us to father.

If you take nothing else away from this chapter, take this: Whether you are single, unsupported, or have the full support of a faithful Catholic husband, the good news is that, if a child falls away from the Faith, you are not helpless in the battle for your sons' souls. You may not have considered that *you can make your prayers more powerful than they are right now.* How? Become a saint! That is not a platitude; it's the plain and simple truth, and it's something we don't hear enough. We hear that we should pray for our children, but we forget that as we ourselves become more holy, more abandoned to God's will, more dead to self, more detached from this world and attached to God, the closer we come to the heart of the Trinity.

The saints in union with God, both in Heaven and on earth, have no barriers between themselves and Christ, and their prayers are explosively powerful. Scripture tells us, "The prayer of the righteous is powerful and effective" (Jas 5:16), so work toward righteousness! Become a saint! What is stopping you? What else matters? There is nothing else that we are ultimately called to do anyway, so get to it. And in the process, you will help to save the souls around you with an overflow of grace in your own soul. God wants not only the sanctity of your sons, after all, but of yourself. Make holiness your mission, and watch what happens to those around you. Miracles of grace follow saints wherever they go.

Which brings me to something I consider crucial and nonnegotiable for all Catholic families, whether intact or not: *make the practice of your faith a joyful one.* Children who see their childhood religion as a source of misery, strife, anxiety, harsh judgments, dour faces, and/or humorlessness will surely turn away from it the first chance they get.

But if your child's experience of the Faith is affirming, loving, merciful, welcoming, and *joyful*, then he will associate his Catholicism with joy. And if he should still stray from the Faith? Well, when the world starts to let him down, disturb him, cast him into darkness, and even eat him alive—which it eventually will, given enough time—he has a firm foundation to come back to someday and a soft place to land.

If, throughout our children's childhoods, we worry and fret and hand-wring for too long, we are not only failing to trust in an all-powerful, all-knowing, all-good God, but we are also telegraphing to our children that we are afraid, or that the world is spinning out of control. As believers in Divine Providence we know that the world is in the hands of our loving Father, and He can be trusted. We do our part, and He does His. Relax and trust Him, and teach your children to do the same.

At every turn, especially when things with our children go wrong, we cling to **hope**, that theological virtue that is not simply "optimism" but rather a belief in the *certainty* of God's promises, and thus we remain in His **joy**.

Let's end our conversation with a few final thoughts . . . .

Chapter Fourteen

Some Final Thoughts

We've come to the end of our conversation together, and although we have discussed many important things, we have left so much more unconsidered.

If I had you in front of me now, if you had gathered up your belongings to head home after our mom-to-mom talk at my kitchen table, I would grab you and put my hands on your shoulders, look you straight in the eye, and tell you the following, from my heart:

Talk to your sons. Keep the lines of communication open—always. Keep your sense of humor no matter what. Never compromise your Catholic Faith, but always live it out. Let your children be able to say of you: "Her faith and her life were never separate." Speak in terms of virtues and not "values." If you are married, stay married and keep your marriage strong. Be a witness for chastity and for marriage in a thirsting, hurting world that needs to see it. In doing so, you will be a beacon for many weary souls, including your own children.

Read the Scriptures and partake of the sacraments often. The Eucharist is the source and summit of the Christian life because the Eucharist is Christ Himself, Body, Blood, Soul, and Divinity. Go to Mass and adoration. Bask in His glory, be with Him, adore Him, consume Him—as He, in turn, consumes you. Go to Confession frequently and take your sons. The graces received there are real. The sanctifying grace of the sacraments is the (literal) life of God, which will carry us to Heaven—and that has been the goal all along.

Do not be afraid. Of anything. God is in control of—and is much bigger than—this world. He cares for you as tenderly and lovingly and personally as you care for your own child—except infinitely more. Pray to Him. Rest in Him. Be at peace. Then do your best and let it go.

Then, I would give you a hug and let you be on your way. You've got sons to raise.

And when night comes, and you look back over the day
and see how fragmentary everything has been,
and how much you planned that has gone undone,
and all the reasons you have to be embarrassed and ashamed:
just take everything exactly as it is,
put it in God's hands
and leave it with Him.

— Saint Teresa Benedicta of the Cross (Edith Stein)

Afterword
Anthony Esolen

(For those boys struggling with same-sex attraction)

In a recent article for *Crisis*, I took to task Fr. James Martin, S.J., for calling it a cause for celebration, when a teenage boy declared to his father, on Thanksgiving, that he was a homosexual. I said that it would be the worst day of the father's life, because he would know that he and his son had failed as a tandem to negotiate the rough rapids of the boy's puberty, and he would also be quite sure that his son had already acted upon his confused feelings. The evil habit would already have reached its tentacles into the boy's flesh and soul.

A good priest then wrote to me to warn me that my words might be misconstrued. He feared that some boy might read them and then be afraid to speak to his father about his sexual doubts and misgivings and confused feelings. The priest is quite correct.

Let me now reassure any boy or young man who may read these words. Talk to your father. Do not talk to a gay man or to your school counselor. If the counselor is a woman, she will know as much about your feelings as I know about being pregnant. If the counselor is a man, he likely has stock in the whole sexual breakdown of our time. Do not talk to your friends, whom you cannot trust to keep your words to themselves. They are, after all, young, as you are, and prone to give way to the impulse of the moment. *Talk to your father.*

Think of how easily and stupidly your body is aroused. You may be sitting in an odd position. You may be horsing around with the dog on the floor. You may be wrestling with your kid brother. You may be taking a shower. Almost anything can trip the trigger. It means nothing.

But you are in the locker room and you steal a shy look at the kid with the muscles. Big deal. You think you are unusual? Every single boy in that locker room has done the same. They still do. You just don't notice it, and there's no reason why you should. You feel some misgivings, though. Let me try to explain what is going on.

Every single culture in the history of the world has been built upon three forms of love. The first is what we have in common with all the animals: it is the most powerful of our natural bonds. It is the love of a mother for her child. The second love gives the first love a haven, and is blessed by God in a special way; it is the love without which children themselves would not exist. That is the love of man and woman in marriage, raised to the height of glory in the marriage of the eternal bridegroom Christ, with his bride, the Church.

The third, we are apt to overlook and neglect. It is the

bond of brother and brother. It is not foundational, as is that of mother and child; it is not an image of the eternal, as is that of bride and groom. It is, however, the bond without which no *culture* comes into existence in the first place, and then survives. It is the bond that builds bridges, tunnels through mountains, raises walls, drains swamps, clears fields, drills wells, fights for the homeland, erects churches and temples, strings the nerves of commerce and power across a continent, and makes a people into a people rather than a confusion of squabbling families.

Is it celebrated in Scripture? It hardly needed to be; it was so taken for granted everywhere. But the answer is yes. We have what a wise friend of mine long ago set before my attention, the "forgotten icon," the band of brothers we know as Christ and the apostles. Jesus was under no illusions about male perfection. He calls Peter "Satan," he expresses impatience with Philip for being so slow to understand him, he rebukes James and John—to whom he has given the jaunty and somewhat unflattering nickname, "Sons of Thunder"—for their ambition; and we need not bother to discuss the hard words he has for the important men of his time. Meanwhile his words to women, though they are frank, are always gentle, even when he tests the faith of the Canaanite woman. Yet Jesus chose men for his apostles.

You see, young man, that Jesus himself was a man, and was drawn to the band of brothers, just as he was drawn to every other good thing in our lives: to the flowers of the desert, to happy feasts, to the love of a kind father, to the sacred songs of his forefathers. Let us then pierce through the confusion of your adolescence and the treachery of our times, and see realities again. What Jesus experienced in his humanity—the boy's attraction to the male band; recall how the boy Jesus remained behind in Jerusalem to trade questions and answers with the learned men?—every boy and young man experiences. Every one of them; it is as natural as breathing. You are *not different from any boy or young man in this regard.* We are all the same.

But your feelings are powerful. Well, flimsy bonds do not move mountains. Of course they are powerful. The football player you admire, he has those feelings too. But in his case, the feelings are satisfied by a powerful and normal and healthy object. He has his football squad, and that both affirms him as a man and clears up his confusions. The difference between you and him is not in the kind of feelings you have, but in his good fortune, to have had those feelings directed aright and satisfied in a way that builds up his identity as a man.

Take yourself out of your particular situation. Imagine that you've grown up in what people would have found normal at most times and in most places. Forget football, baseball, and other sports that require some special skill that you may not have. Imagine that you live on a farm. All your life long you have been out in the fields with boys and men, working, laughing, quarreling, sweating, eating, playing. You have never been in doubt for a moment about your sex and your belonging with others of your kind, because that's all you have known. You would have the same ordinary feelings that other boys have, yet they wouldn't be a source of pain or fear. They couldn't be. Every day you will have been affirmed as a masculine being, just from the work you do. You could have been born with exactly the same genetic makeup, but in that world, a harsh but healthy world, you would have had no doubts about what you were.

Be assured. You are the same, you are one of us.

And your sexual feelings? Your arousal? Meaningless, and transitory, unless you put the feelings into action. Don't do that. Think: "This feeling is stupid." Do not take it too seriously. Some people cannot walk across a bridge without thinking of doing something stupid. Meaningless, and transitory. Your sexual feelings during the teenage years are on overdrive. A picture of Michelangelo's *David* will set you off. Big deal. Be patient. Do not do anything sexual with anybody. By all means stay away from porn. On the whole matter of purity, see a good priest and take his advice. About your feelings, don't let them preoccupy you. Consider it a part of growing up.

But if you are worried, talk to your father. If you have done something dumb, something you are ashamed of, by all means go to your father. You may be astounded by the old man's wisdom. He will have seen a lot more than you will believe. Go to him. Do not go to the school counselor; do not go to any adult who has a vested interest in your *failing*. Talk to your father.

And remember what I say. Your real need is for masculine affirmation, so often expressed in a broadly physical way—

think of a big bunch of coal miners showering after a day under the earth. This is ordinary. Friendship, that is the need. Your father can help you there too. Talk to him.

Originally appeared in *Crisis Magazine* online,
October 25, 2017
crisismagazine.com/2017/tak-to-your-father
(Used with permission)

Endnotes

1 Olmsted, Bishop Thomas J., http://intothebreach.org.

2 http://www.vatican.va/roman_curia/pontifical_councils/family/documents/rc_pc_family_doc_08121995_human-sexuality_en.html.

3 https://www.catholicculture.org/culture/library/dictionary/index.cfm?id=33669.

4 Sexuality Information and Education Council of the United States.

5 After the first edition of this book, my daughter told me: "Mom! That advice didn't work with my son!" He was two at the time, and she found her own excellent solution to break the habit: She put him in overalls over a one-piece every day for a few weeks, so that he couldn't "get to it"! Another suggestion: Make sure you check with your child's doctor for possible infection, in case his constant scratching and adjusting has a medical cause.

6 Clinton, Hillary, floor of the US Senate, 2004, https://

www.youtube.com/watch?v=6I1-r1YgK9I.

⁷ I wrote (and warned) about this long ago: http://little-catholicbubble.blogspot.com/2011/08/catholics-your-misguided-compassion.html.

⁸ https://www.adflegal.org/issues/religious-freedom/conscience.

⁹ https://www.gov.uk/how-to-annul-marriage/when-you-can-annul-a-marriage.

¹⁰ Sister Lucia, one of the three children at Fatima who saw our Blessed Mother, wrote this late in her life: "The final battle between the Lord and the kingdom of Satan will be about marriage and the family." https://www.catholicnewsagency.com/news/fatima-visionary-predicted-final-battle-would-be-over-marriage-family-17760.

¹¹ Lowery, Mark, http://www.catholiceducation.org/en/marriage-and-family/sexuality/chastity-before-marriage-a-fresh-perspective.html.

¹² Spenceley, Arleen, *The Tampa Bay Times*, March 13, 2015, http://www.tampabay.com/news/perspective/perspective-how-chastity-can-lead-to-good-sex/2221250.

¹³ Sheen, Father Fulton J., "Comments on the Report of the Federal Council of Churches of Christ in America," The American Birth Control League's *Birth Control Review*, Volume XV, Number 4 (April 1931), p. 143.

¹⁴ Pope Paul VI, http://w2.vatican.va/content/paul-vi/en/encyclicals/documents/hf_p-vi_enc_25071968_humanae-vitae.html.

15 *Planned Parenthood of Southeastern Pennsylvania, et al. vs. Robert P. Casey, et al.* Can be found at http://caselaw.findlaw.com/us-supreme-court/505/833.html.

16 https://www.reddit.com/r/NoFap/comments/23yg85/ultimate_benefits_thread/ [Warning: contains explicit/offensive language].

17 Joycelyn Elders, "Abstinence," Penn & Teller: Bullshit! (Showtime), June 5, 2006.

18 Flock, Elizabeth, "Devout Catholics Have Better Sex, Study Says," *US News and World Report*, July 17, 2013, http://www.usnews.com/news/articles/2013/07/17/devout-catholics-have-better-sex.

19 Suramek, Mae, http://plainjaneactivism.blogspot.com. Note: Sometime between the first and second editions of this book, the blogger took down that particular description from her sidebar.

20 Esolen, Anthony, May 21, 2016, *"Remember the Boys,"* https://www.thecatholicthing.org/2016/05/21/remember-the-boys/.

21 Savage, Deborah, "The Nature of Woman in Relation to Man," *Logos* (Winter 2015): 89 & 91.

22 Barack Obama's votes on the "Born-Alive Infants Protection" bills are on the record and searchable. This article includes an overview of his position and audio of an Illinois Senate hearing: http://www.lifenews.com/2012/08/23/new-audio-surfaces-of-obama-defending-infanticide-in-illinois/.

23 Jones, Tim, "Barack Obama: Mother not just another

girl from Kansas," *Chicago Tribune*, March 27, 2007, http://www.webcitation.org/66cdqjbue.

[24] https://en.wikipedia.org/wiki/Ann_Dunham.

[25] To read the young men's complete answers, go to: http://littlecatholicbubble.blogspot.com/p/raising-chaste-catholic-men-young-men.html.

[26] http://littlecatholicbubble.blogspot.com/2014/12/my-mother-in-law-carols-conversion.html.

Resources

For all the information below plus more resources and links not included here, simply go to this address: http://littlecatholicbubble.blogspot.com/p/raising-chaste-catholic-men-appendix-and.html

THEOLOGY OF THE BODY (TOB)

YOU: Life, Love, and the Theology of the Body by Brian Butler, Jason Evert, and Crystalina Evert
Theology of the Body in One Hour by Jason Evert
Theology of the Body for Beginners by Christopher West
Good News about Sex and Marriage by Christopher West
http://thetheologyofthebody.com

CONTRACEPTION

One of the best overviews I've read online:
http://www.thepublicdiscourse.com/2016/08/17559/

And a great book resource:
Sex au Naturel: What It Is and Why It's Good for Your Marriage by Patrick Coffin

NATURAL FAMILY PLANNING (NFP)

The basic science of it:
http://littlecatholicbubble.blogspot.com/2011/03/the-natural-family-planning-post.html

Why it is not simply "Catholic contraception":
http://littlecatholicbubble.blogspot.com/2011/03/important-follow-up-to-natural-family.html

From the US bishops:
http://www.usccb.org/issues-and-action/marriage-and-family/natural-family-planning/catholic-teaching/upload/Chastity.pdf

NATURAL LAW

What We Can't Not Know by Professor J. Budziszewski
On the Meaning of Sex by Professor J. Budziszewski

"GAY MARRIAGE"

For many legal and social implications:
http://littlecatholicbubble.blogspot.com/p/how-does-gay-marriage-affect-you-anyway.html

Was Jesus silent on gay "marriage"?
http://www.catholiclane.com/was-jesus-really-silent-on-same-sex-marriage/

Do the children have a say?
http://littlecatholicbubble.blogspot.com/2013/06/should-children-sit-down-and-shut-up.html

TRANSGENDERISM

http://www.thepublicdiscourse.com/2016/05/17041/
http://www.thepublicdiscourse.com/2016/06/17166/

PORNOGRAPHY

Help for pornography addiction:
http://catholicmenconquerporn.com/courses/overcome-porn-addiction
http://www.angelicwarfareconfraternity.org
Internet filter:
http://www.covenanteyes.com/

SCRUPULOSITY

http://scrupulousanonymous.org
Understanding Scrupulosity: Questions, Helps, and Encouragement by Rev. Thomas Santa, CSsR

BOOKS FOR CHILDREN

For teaching our younger children how to avoid bad pictures:
Good Pictures Bad Pictures: Porn-Proofing Today's Young Kids by Kristen A. Jenson and Gail Poyner

Sex and reproduction:
The Joyful Mysteries of Life by Catherine and Bernard Scherrer
Wonderfully Made! Babies by Ellen Giangiordano

BOOKS FOR TEENS

Theology of His Body / Theology of Her Body by Jason Evert

General apologetics, good for skeptical teens:
The Prove It! books by Amy Welborn

PRAYER AND HOLINESS

Into Your Hands, Father: Abandoning Ourselves to the God Who Loves Us by Father Wilfrid Stinissen

He Leadeth Me by Father Walter Ciszek

Spiritual Passages: The Psychology of Spiritual Development by Father Benedict Groeschel

The Power of Silence by Cardinal Robert Sarah

Searching for and Maintaining Peace: A Small Treatise on Peace of Heart by Father Jacques Philippe

How to Pray Always by Father Raoul Plus

Prayer Works! Getting a Grip on Catholic Spirituality by Matthew Leonard

The Contemplative Rosary by Dan Burke and Connie Rossini

Conversation with Christ: The Teaching of St. Teresa of Avila about Personal Prayer by Peter Thomas Rohrbach

IF YOU EVER FEEL LIKE A FAILURE AS A MOTHER

I have felt your pain!

http://littlecatholicbubble.blogspot.com/2011/10/why-i-never-should-have-had-eight.html

CONTACT ME

Leila@LeilaMiller.net

Will your children's Catholic faith and morals survive adolescence?

Steer your children safely through the temptations and turbulence of their teen years with sound, practical advice for solving—or preventing—the problems that can trouble even the best-raised teens. *Forming Character in Adolescents*, by Dr Rudolf Allers, arose from a series of articles for priests in the late 1930s intending (in the author's words) to "bring together reliable statements of psychology and the immutable principles of sound philosophy" as the "very best means of practical" advice for Catholic parents. *(Hardbound, 188 pages)*

This is the ONLY psychology book we've ever seen with an Imprimatur!